# The Book of Romans Commentary

James Battell

Published by James Battell, 2024.

While every precaution has been taken in the preparation of this book, the publisher assumes no responsibility for errors or omissions, or for damages resulting from the use of the information contained herein.

THE BOOK OF ROMANS COMMENTARY

**First edition. February 2, 2024.**



ISBN: 979-8224091416

Written by James Battell.

# Also by James Battell

The Shocking History of the Jesuits (The Society of Jesus)

King James I of England: The King The Vatican Could Not Kill

The Hidden Truth About Freemasonry, The Catholic Church, And The Illuminati

Bible Prophecy Made Simple For Serious Students of Scripture

Did The Catholic Church Order Abraham Lincoln's Assassination?

Is Calvinism and the Doctrines of Grace Biblical?

The Book of Genesis Commentary (Chapters 1-11)

The Book of Genesis Commentary (Chapters 1-11)

Watchman Nee, Witness Lee, and Living Stream Ministry: A Critical Analysis of Their Identity as Cult or Church

What Is Speaking In Tongues And Is It Still For Today?

Ephesians KJV Bible Commentary

The Book of Romans Commentary

Philemon Bible Study (Slavery In Scripture)

Turbulent Thrones: Charles vs. Cromwell's Epic Struggle for England's Soul

The Holy Ghost Within The Trinity

Papal Infallibility or Insanity?

The Immaculate Conception ("Deception")

# CHAPTER 1

VERSES 1-7: "Paul, a servant of Jesus Christ, called *to be* an apostle, separated unto the gospel of God, (Which he had promised afore by his prophets in the holy scriptures,) Concerning his Son Jesus Christ our Lord, which was made of the seed of David according to the flesh; And declared *to be* the Son of God with power, according to the spirit of holiness, by the resurrection from the dead: By whom we have received grace and apostleship, for obedience to the faith among all nations, for his name: Among whom are ye also the called of Jesus Christ: To all that be in Rome, beloved of God, called *to be* saints: Grace to you and peace from God our Father, and the Lord Jesus Christ."

Seven, in numerology, is very important and these seven verses open Paul's masterpiece. Romans is a remarkable book. This epistle is so deep and so profound and spiritually so rich that most teachers won't even touch it. But I, Lord willing, will approach it with reverence, with care, and humility.

In chapter 1 verse 1, Paul says he was a servant of the Lord Jesus Christ who was then called to be an apostle. Nobody called Paul to be an apostle, and nobody laid their hands on Paul in order for him to become an apostle. He was chosen directly from the Lord Jesus Christ in Acts chapter 9. He also says from chapter 1, verse 1, he was separated until the gospel of God, meaning he was now set apart to be a servant and an apostle. He wrote the book, literally, when it comes to how Christians should live and function. What this man forgot, we shall never know, meaning he learnt everything, he knew everything. He wasn't sinless, but he was a remarkable man of God, and we can learn so much from the apostle Paul.

In verse 2, Paul mentions the Holy Scriptures, the Jewish Tanach. Paul was a Jew of the Jews. He knew the Old Testament inside out. And he knew that religion could not save him, and religion cannot save you. You must be born again.

In verse 3, he says Jesus was made of the seed of David. The Lord Jesus Christ has two natures: He is God, He is divine, He is eternal; and at the same time, He is also man. In 4 B.C., He was born, and as the Son of Man, He is in the line of King David. He is the Jewish Messiah.

In verse 4, he says the Son of God was declared with power, according to the spirit of holiness, by the resurrection from the dead. The most profound event in the history of mankind is the resurrection of the Lord Jesus Christ. So, the Lord Jesus is mentioned in verse 1, as is God the Father, and in verse 4, the Holy Spirit is mentioned. Three in one, one in three, and the One in the middle died for me. That's the Trinity, of course.

Okay, so moving on through the Epistle to the Romans, and during the last broadcast, we found God the Son in chapter 1, verse 1, and God the Father in chapter 1, verse 1. We also found God the Holy Spirit in chapter 1, verse 4. The Triune God created the universe and the Triune God resurrected the Lord

Jesus Christ. John, chapter 2, the Lord Jesus resurrects Himself from the dead and in Galatians, chapter 1, God the Father resurrected the Lord Jesus Christ from the dead. Here, in verse 4, the Holy Spirit is credited with the resurrection of the Lord Jesus Christ. So each member of the Godhead resurrected the Lord Jesus Christ.

In verses 2 and 3, Paul says that the Old Testament Scriptures promised the coming of the Jewish Messiah. There are over 68 prophecies concerning the Lord Jesus Christ, written hundreds if not thousands of years before He was even born; 68 prophecies written about a King and His kingdom. The King, of course, is Jesus Christ. And the kingdom is the kingdom of God. Yes, 41 authors living on 3 continents over 1600 years apart wrote the Bible, but God inspired them to write the Holy Scriptures. They wrote what He told them to write. The Bible is divine in origin, not human. You can trust it totally and completely.

And we discovered from chapter 1, verse 3, how Jesus was made after the seed of David. God became man in the person of Jesus Christ. God, of course, is eternal; He is omnipresent; He is omnipotent; and He is omniscient. But He chose to enter into the human race and become a man and die for the sins of the world. In Hebrews chapter 2, verse 18, the word of God says the following: **"For in that he himself hath suffered being tempted, he is able to succour them that are tempted."** So the Lord Jesus Christ really does know what it's like to live on this earth, to suffer on this earth and to die on this earth. Do you know the Lord Jesus Christ? If you don't, you can know

Him. Just call on His name, and He will reach out and He will grab you.

No other religious person, no other deity, went through what He went through. He was a King. He came down from Heaven to earth. And He paid for all of our sins on the cross. We saw it in verse 4. The Son of God was declared with power by the resurrection from the dead. He is God and He is man.

So, we are still in the first seven verses of the Epistle to the Romans. Like I said from the beginning of this broadcast, this book is very deep and very profound. And we have discovered so much during the first two broadcasts of this new series of recordings, looking at the Epistle to the Romans.

In verse 5, he says, **"we have received grace and apostleship, for obedience to the faith among all nations, for his name"**. Peter, John, and Andrew, and James, no doubt, are in his mind. Paul was a very humble man. Chapter 1, verse 1, he says he was a servant. But for the Name's sake, of the Lord Jesus, they have received the office of an apostle. Not only did the apostles write the New Testament, but they did many, many miracles. Peter and Paul resurrected dead people. They cast out devils from unsaved people. They were eyewitnesses to the majesty of the Lord Jesus Christ. Yes, Paul was saved post the crucifixion, but he saw the Lord Jesus Christ on the road to Damascus. And 2 Corinthians 12 tells us that he was taken up to the third Heaven. That is where the Lord God of the Bible resides.

In verse 6, he says, **"Among whom are ye also the called of Jesus Christ"**. These people are Christians. They are followers. They are disciples of the Lord Jesus Christ, the God-man.

In verse 7, he says, **"To all that be in Rome, beloved of God, called *to be* saints"**. Once you are born again, you are automatically made a saint, by God, by the new birth. No church can make you a saint; only God can make you a saint. And these saints in Rome are beloved of God. With the Roman empire pretty much governing most of the world at this point in the history of mankind, Paul knew that if he could make it to Rome, not only would more people be saved as a result of his preaching, but through his preaching he could reach out to the rest of the world and see millions of people saved by the preaching of the cross. But, as of writing this epistle, he has still to make it to Rome. That's his goal. Rome, as I say, was the capital of the entire world when he wrote this epistle. If he can make it there, he can make it anywhere for the Lord Jesus Christ and His glory and for His name's sake.

So, moving on through the Epistle to the Romans. And during the last few broadcasts, I showed you how much material was found in the first 7 verses. And seven and also eight are very important numbers when it comes to the subject of numerology.

But let's start this broadcast in verse 8: **"First, I thank my God through Jesus Christ for you all, that your faith is spoken of throughout the whole world."**

This has got to be one of the most profound statements in the Scriptures. He has written to the Romans from verse 7, and he says their faith is spoken of throughout the entire world. Can you imagine that? When you get saved, there should be a change within you. Not only will you know it, but people around you will see it.

But these people go one step further than that. Their faith is known abroad and Paul quite rightly is commending them for such a faith.

Also of interest to me, Paul says **"I thank my God"**. This is very Pauline. In his epistles, he will normally say the Lord Jesus Christ is **"our Saviour"**. But here, and in other parts of the New Testament, he does say "my God". And also, you will find in this epistle **"my gospel"**. Paul was a Jew of the Jews, and here the Jewish apostle is writing to the Gentiles. There were some Jews at Rome at this stage, I believe, but by and large, he is speaking to Gentile people and he has still retained some of that Jewishness. **"My God, my Saviour, my gospel."**

**VERSES 9-10: "For God is my witness, whom I serve with my spirit in the gospel of his Son, that without ceasing I make mention of you always in my prayers; Making request, if by any means now at length I might have a prosperous journey by the will of God to come unto you."**

That was his plan, like I say. He wanted to make it to Rome and once he made it to Rome, he knew that the word of God would go out to all of the earth and mankind would be forever changed.

**VERSES 11-12: "For I long to see you, that I may impart unto you some spiritual gift, to the end ye may be established; That is, that I may be comforted together with you by the mutual faith both of you and me."**

Can you appreciate what you've just heard here? Paul has been saved for x amount of years. He is going to write half of the New Testament. He has been to the third Heaven and back, and yet he is saying that these people in Rome have something that he wants to share with. They have a common faith in the Lord Jesus Christ. But much more than that, he wants to visit them, fellowship with them, and impart some spiritual gift to them. This group of Bible-believing Christians must have been very precious and very special and very rare in the eyes of the apostle Paul. And like I say, his goal now is to get to Rome. It's not going to be easy, because the Roman emperors at the time of him writing this epistle and their secret police were very much against Christianity. Why? Because they were monotheist. They were no threat to the state. But they would not worship false pagan gods. They would not worship their idols, their images. So Paul has to make it to Rome. But it's not going to be easy.

So, continuing on through the Epistle to the Romans. And, if you haven't already appreciated, chapter 1 is filled with good material. There is so much substance in the Book of the Romans, but chapter 1 is amazing.

Let's start this broadcast from verse 13: **"Now I would not have you ignorant, brethren, that oftentimes I purposed to**

**come unto you, (but was let hitherto,) that I might have some fruit among you also, even as among other Gentiles."**

This early community must have been basking in the finished work of the Lord Jesus Christ. He is desperate to get to Rome, like I say. He wants to fellowship with them. He wants to worship with them. He wants to be with them. Their testimonies were magnificent. But verse 13 makes it very clear that he wasn't able to get there. He wanted to travel there on many occasions. But it wasn't always possible. Why not? Because the devil was always against the apostle Paul. If you are saved, if you have an active life-changing ministry, the devil is always going to be on your back. The apostle Paul was the greatest man that ever lived, and yet he could not shake Satan off his back. He had to live every single day like it was his last day and the Lord gave him the grace to do so.

Look at verse 14: **"I am debtor both to the Greeks, and to the Barbarians; both to the wise, and to the unwise."**

Please turn to 1 Corinthians chapter 9. If you come across a piece of Scripture which isn't always clear, you need to go to another piece of Scripture and compare Scripture with Scripture. That's one of the cardinal rules of hermeneutics. Look at 1 Corinthians, chapter 9. Let's start in verse 19: **"For though I be free from all *men*, yet have I made myself servant unto all, that I might gain the more. And unto the Jews I became as a Jew, that I might gain the Jews; to them that are under the law, as under the law, that I might gain them that are under the law; To them that are without law, as without law, (being not without law to God, but under**

**the law to Christ,) that I might gain them that are without law. To the weak became I as weak, that I might gain the weak: I am made all things to all men, that I might by all means save some."**

Please go back to Romans chapter 1. What we have just seen is in 1 Corinthians 9 further expounds what we just discovered in Romans chapter 1, verse 14. He was a servant to the Jews and also to the Gentiles. Chapter 1, verse 1: **"Paul, a servant of Jesus Christ"** meaning he was all things to all people that he might save some. In today's world, we would call Paul a people's person, and he did it to perfection. Also, from verse 14, Greeks would be Gentiles, as would barbarians to some extent. Some people are going to be wise, and some people are going to be unwise. But, until you are saved, you are outside of the kingdom of God.

So, moving on through the Epistle to the Romans, and in the last broadcast I showed you how the apostle Paul lowered himself to fit in with every type of person. We found from verse 14 how he was a debtor both to the Greeks, the educated people of his day, and also to the barbarians, the uneducated people, the illiterate people, the lower of the lower-class people. He was all things to all people, including the Jews. He says in the later chapters of Romans how he wished he was accursed for the sake of his people that they might be saved. This man had a huge heart. What this man forgot we will never know. Like I say, he wrote the book and he set the example as to how all Bible-believing Christians should live. He was a one-off man.

But we don't worship the apostle Paul. We worship the triune God. Our faith is in the triune God, not Paul, not Peter, not James, not John. Not even in the Bible. We are saved by our faith in the Lord Jesus Christ alone. But in order to grow in grace and be an effective Bible-believing Christian, we have to read the Bible, we have to believe the Bible, and we have to apply the Bible and what it clearly states to every aspect of our lives.

So let's start today's broadcast in verse 15: **"So, as much as in me is, I am ready to preach the gospel to you that are at Rome also."**

At this point in the ministry of the apostle Paul, he had travelled around most of the Roman Empire. He wrote the Epistle to the Romans around 56 A.D. And you can feel the anticipation building up. He has got to get to Rome. These people are so unique. They have an excellent testimony. Unlike the Corinthians that were carnal, unlike the Galatians that were legalistic, these people were the best of the best, and he has got to get to Rome.

Please look at verse 16: **"For I am not ashamed of the gospel of Christ: for it is the power of God unto salvation to every one that believeth; to the Jew first, and also to the Greek."**

Yet another profound statement. Two points from verse 16 which really stand out: number 1, the apostle Paul was not ashamed of the gospel of the Lord Jesus Christ, and number 2, he says the power of the gospel was available to everyone that believeth, to the Jew and also to the Greek. Meaning, quite simply, that if the Jew believed on Jesus he/she would be saved, and if the Greek believed on the Lord Jesus, he/she would be saved as well. The Lord Jesus Christ died for the sins of the whole world, without exception. But, only those that believe on Him are going to be saved.

So, we are still in the first chapter of the Book of the Romans. And I showed you all from verse 16 last time how the apostle Paul at this late stage of his life was not ashamed of the gospel of the Lord Jesus Christ. He wasn't perfect, he wasn't sinless. But at this stage, he had grown to become a mature, well-grounded, Bible-believing Christian. Timothy, on the other hand, half the age of the apostle Paul, was ashamed. Therefore, if you are a Bible-believing Christian and you're not yet confident enough to proclaim the gospel of the Lord Jesus Christ, don't worry. It will come all in good time. Paul had decades to perfect his walk with the Lord Jesus Christ.

Also, I want to quickly squeeze in one important footnote from verse 16. Paul says that the power of the gospel could save Jew and Greek. Please turn to John chapter 6. Scripture with Scripture. Please look at verse 44, Jesus speaking: **"No man can come to me, except the Father which hath sent me draw him: and I will raise him up at the last day".** This is a favourite passage for the Calvinists. And they read this verse, and they normally stop there. Please turn to John chapter 12. Again, Scripture with Scripture to understand what the Bible clearly states, not what you've been told the Bible teaches. Please look at verse 32, Jesus speaking again: **"And I, if I be lifted up from the earth, will draw all *men* unto me."** You can't come to the Father unless the Father draws you to Him, the Father being

God of course. And here, God the Son says **"I will draw all men unto me."** When did this happen? When he was lifted up from the earth. First of all, the resurrection; secondly, at the ascension. He has drawn all men unto Him.

Some people say, well, he hasn't granted repentance to everybody. Please turn to Acts chapter 5. Again, Scripture with Scripture. Acts chapter 5. Please look at verse 31: **"Him hath God exalted with his right hand *to be* a Prince and a Saviour, for to give repentance to Israel, and forgiveness of sins."** God has already granted repentance to the Jews. Please turn to Acts chapter 11. We are not finished yet. Look at verse 18: **"When they heard these things, they held their peace, and glorified God, saying, Then hath God also to the Gentiles granted repentance unto life."** So, here the Gentiles have also been granted repentance unto life.

One more Scripture please. Go to 2 Corinthians chapter 5. Look at verse 19 please: **"To wit, that God was in Christ, reconciling the world unto himself, not imputing their trespasses unto them; and hath committed unto us the word of reconciliation."** Look at verse 20: **"Now then we are ambassadors for Christ, as though God did beseech *you* by us: we pray *you* in Christ's stead, be ye reconciled to God."**

John chapter 6 showed you the source of the new birth. God the Father drawing sinners unto His Son. John chapter 12 showed you how the Lord Jesus Christ has now drawn all men unto Himself. Romans chapter 1, verse 1, God the Son is mentioned, and God the Father. Chapter 1, verse 4, God the Holy Spirit is mentioned in reference to the resurrection of the Lord Jesus Christ. Once again, the triune God are found throughout the entire Bible.

But my main point from verse 16 is that Christ is the power to salvation for those that believe. Acts chapter 5, God has granted repentance to the Jews. Acts chapter 11, God has granted repentance to the Gentiles. 2 Corinthians chapter 5, he says: **"be ye reconciled to God"**, the apostle Paul of course. God has drawn all men unto Himself. But what does verse 16 say, one more time: **"for it is the power of God unto salvation to every one that believeth"**. Believe, trust, receive the Lord Jesus Christ!

So, let's conclude this broadcast in verse 17: **"For therein is the righteousness of God revealed from faith to faith: as it is written, The just shall live by faith."**

Once you are born again, you have been justified and, therefore, as a just man or woman, you now live by faith. Not a blind faith; you have the Holy Scriptures to read, to meditate, and to obey. And you have the triune God living within you. **"The just shall live by faith"**. You got saved by believing on the Lord Jesus Christ. Now you live and function by your faith in the Lord Jesus Christ.

Okay, so continuing on through the Epistle to the Romans. And last time we finished at verse 17, where the apostle Paul was quoting from the Old Testament Book of Habakkuk, and the Scripture says, **"The just shall live by faith."** Once you are saved, you walked and live by faith. Never mind prophesies, never mind visions, never mind what he said or what she said.

What sayeth the Scripture. You are saved by your faith in the Lord Jesus Christ and what He did for you, not what you do for Him. Our faith isn't a blind faith. For those of us that have been saved, our lives have been totally transformed by a Man who lived 2,000 years ago. If you want to know the will of God for your life, you need to read the word of God each and every day.

So, let's start today's broadcast, if we may, in verse 18: **"For the wrath of God is revealed from heaven against all ungodliness and unrighteousness of men, who hold the truth in unrighteousness; Because that which may be known of God is manifest in them; for God hath shewed** *it* **unto them."**

There's two parts to this piece of Scripture, from verses 20, 21 and 22, right the way down to 23, 24, the apostle Paul says that the creation of the universe is evidence of a Creator. A house doesn't build itself. A watch doesn't build itself. There's always a creator. A design always presupposes a designer. And the designer, in this case, is the Lord God of the Bible.

But from verses 18 and 19, Paul is focusing on the wrath of God abiding on mankind, in relation to his conscience. When you sin, your conscience tells you that you have sinned. That comes from Heaven, not from man. You were made in the image of God. Your conscience comes from Heaven and, therefore, when you die and stand before Him you cannot say to the Lord of the universe, I didn't know it was wrong to steal or murder or commit adultery. Your heart convicted you when you sinned. But Scripture tells us that men love darkness rather than light. Therefore, this is a heart issue, not a head issue.

So, through your conscience you know there is a Creator, but due to your love of sin and your hatred of God, you choose to ignore Him and suppress what you do know of Him through unrighteousness, through carnality, through riotous living. Therefore, when you die and stand in His presence, you won't be found not guilty, but you will be found guilty. And you will go into the lake of fire which burns forever and forever. He died for you. He has atoned for your sins, but you didn't want Him. You chose to reject Him and embrace everything and anything except Him.

So, we are still very much in chapter 1 of the Epistle to the Romans. As I've said from the beginning of these broadcasts, this book is very deep. And this book is quite possibly the greatest book in the entire Bible. Yes, Genesis told us about creation. Yes, the gospels told us about our blessed Saviour, the Lord Jesus Christ. But this book tells us how man functions. And this book tells us why men do what they do. And this book also tells us how the Lord deals with unrighteousness and sin. This book is very deep, very profound. And, like I say, most Bible-believing teachers rarely, if ever, study and teach the Book of Romans.

So, Lord willing, let's continue on as I go through these series of broadcasts, and I start, in this broadcast for today, in verses 20:21: **"For the invisible things of him from the creation of the world are clearly seen, being understood by the things that are made, even his eternal power and Godhead; so that** they are without excuse: Because that, when they knew God, they glorified *him* not as God, neither were thankful; but became vain in their imaginations, and their foolish heart was darkened."

In Genesis chapter 6, the Lord said that man's heart, his imaginations, were only evil continually. So, He sends the flood to destroy the earth. If God wanted to, He could destroy everybody living today.

People sometimes say, "Why doesn't the Lord intervene and deal with this person or that person, or this sin or that sin?" Well, if He did, you would be destroyed and I would be destroyed. But, thankfully, He is a loving and merciful and understanding Saviour. But verses 20 and 21 are completely and totally damning when it comes to man's accountability in the eyes of the Lord. Verses 18 and 19 dealt with the conscience of mankind, verses 20 and 21 are now focusing on the creation of the world. Like I said, a creation always presupposes a Creator. Verse 20 says that mankind understands that God is God. Even the invisible things of Him are understood by mankind in general. But, instead of thanking Him and worshipping Him they do the complete opposite.

Look at verses 22-23: **"Professing themselves to be wise, they became fools, And changed the glory of the uncorruptible God into an image made like to corruptible man, and to birds, and fourfooted beasts, and creeping things."**

The children of Israel for decades, if not centuries, had the problem of idolatry. Let's build us an image and worship it.

Aaron fell into that sin and subsequently died as a result of that sin. Mankind must believe in something, and mankind must have an image to worship. But verse 17, Paul told you **"The just shall live by faith"**, not sight. Images, which are then accredited to represent the God of the Bible, are prohibited in both Testaments. God hates it. Why do you think there are no accounts of how the Lord Jesus Christ looked? Because God doesn't want people painting pictures of Him and turning around and telling people that is what Jesus looked like. No, He is far too beautiful, He is far too holy, He is far too righteous to be penned by a hand of a carnal artist. God does not want that. And these people found here in verses 20 and 21 and 22 think they are wise, but in essence they are fools and God despises these people.

During the last broadcast, we looked at the Lord's condemnation of sinful man. Man in accountable to the Lord through creation and through his conscience. But instead of man worshipping the Lord of the Bible, he creates animals. He creates images, and he worships the creation of the Lord, rather than the Creator, who is blessed forever. Amen. And God is a jealous God. The Lord did not make mankind in order for mankind to ignore Him and create gods in their own image. Man was made in the image of the triune God. And when God's judgment comes, it's going to come very hard and very fast. So, make sure you are on the right side of the issue here. You cannot be impartial when it comes to the issue of who the triune God is. You are either for Him or you are against Him. It's as simple as that. But these people here are condemned clearly for ignoring the Lord, for creating false images and worshipping them instead of the Lord God of the Bible. Idolatry, pure and simple. And He hates it.

So what happens when mankind rejects the Lord and goes his own way? Look at verses 24-25: **"Wherefore God also gave them up to uncleanness through the lusts of their own hearts, to dishonour their own bodies between themselves: Who changed the truth of God into a lie, and worshipped and served the creature more than the Creator, who is blessed for ever. Amen."**

Please turn to Ephesians chapter 4. Scripture with Scripture. Ephesians chapter 4. Look at verse 19: **"Who being past feeling have given themselves over unto lasciviousness, to work all uncleanness with greediness."** When man turns from the Lord, and continues to turn from the Lord, the Lord gives man up to his sin. But before the Lord gives him up to his sin, he has already given himself up to sin. Found here in Ephesians chapter 4, verse 19. God waits and He waits and He waits. He is not willing that any should perish. He takes no pleasure in the death of the wicked. But if mankind continues to harden his heart and if mankind continues to go his own way, found here in Ephesians 4:19, the Lord says, fine, I will now give you up to uncleanness. And once He gives you up to uncleanness, there is no going back. You are finished.

So, we are still in Romans chapter 1. The last time we looked at verses 24 and 25 and we also saw from Ephesians chapter 4 how man, first of all, gives himself over to a reprobate mind. And if he continues to live in that way of life, the Lord gives him up completely and totally and permanently. And once God does that, there's no going back for you. You are now dead in your sins and forever separated from the Lord God of the Bible. That's your choice, not His. You have a free will, as did Adam, as did Eve. So, when you die and stand before Him, you only have yourself to blame, pure and simple.

So let's start today's broadcast in verse 26, and the theme has not changed. Man has abandoned God, and God has given man up to his sin. What happens when this occurs? Verses 26-27, please: **"For this cause God gave them up unto vile affections: for even their women did change the natural use into that which is against nature: And likewise also the men, leaving the natural use of the woman, burned in their lust one toward another; men with men working that which is unseemly, and receiving in themselves that recompence of their error which was meet."**

Paul goes right to the heart of the issue. Women, first of all, are given over to their sin. And they embrace in same-sex relations, known today as lesbianism. Completely against nature, according to the apostle Paul and found very clearly in both Testaments. Also, for women to be singled out as being given over to this type of sin underscores, once again, just how deep and endemic sin is.

Normally, it's men that fall into sin and they corrupt women. But here Paul says that women have also fallen into sin, and they too are going to corrupt their male counterparts. Women fell into sin here with lesbianism, and in verse 27 men are now lusting after one another. Homosexuality, as it's known today. But the Bible calls it sodomy. Not only does the apostle Paul say that women with women and men with men is against nature, but he also says that they will receive in themselves their recompense of the error which is meet, meaning judgment is going to come on them.

The Lord destroyed Sodom and Gomorrah for this very thing. If He did it then back in the Old Testament, He's going to do it again at His return. The Lord is holy, the Lord is righteous. He made women for men, not men for men and not women for women. Man and woman produce child. That is natural, and that is nature with a capital N.

So we are nearing the end of chapter 1 of the Epistle to the Romans. And if you haven't yet realised, this is a very controversial book. Hence, why most Bible-believing Christians and teachers rarely delve into it and teach it and preach it and present it to their audience. It's controversial. It's not politically correct to believe and to proclaim what is found in this part of the New Testament.

Last time, we saw the Lord giving men and women up to their sin, and at the end of verse 27, Paul says these people are going to receive the recompense for the error of their ways. AIDS, gonorrhoea and syphilis are just some of the consequences of mankind living a lifestyle which the Lord hates and detests.

He can save people out of any sin imaginable, but you have to come to Him and say, Lord, please be merciful to me, a sinner. The just shall live by faith. But you have to call out to Him and beg Him to save you, and He will change you the moment He grabs you, and He will change you from within. And you will now live for the Lord Jesus Christ. Things that you once did in your past that you loved, you are now going to hate. And things you once hated, you are now going to love. It's a paradox, of course. But that is what the new nature does to a saved man or a saved woman. As I say, He will change you from within. He makes dead men alive.

Look at verses 28-32 for this broadcast, please: **"And even as they did not like to retain God in** *their* **knowledge, God gave them over to a reprobate mind, to do those things which are not convenient; Being filled with all unrighteousness, fornication, wickedness, covetousness, maliciousness; full of envy, murder, debate, deceit, malignity; whisperers, Backbiters, haters of God, despiteful, proud, boasters, inventors of evil things, disobedient to parents, Without understanding, covenantbreakers, without natural affection, implacable, unmerciful: Who knowing the judgment of God, that they which commit such things are worthy of death, not only do the same, but have pleasure in them that do them."**

These verses are pretty much a comprehensive list of sins which come from the heart. Like I said, this is a heart issue, not a head issue. Your heart is desperately wicked pre the new birth. He starts in verses 26 and 27 looking at sodomy and lesbianism, and he condemns it. In verses 29, 30, 31 he opens it up even more. People without natural affection are paedophiles, backbiters, haters of God, modern-day atheists found everywhere, disobedient to parents, children now divorcing their parents. Fornication, premarital sex. And by 32, the apostle Paul says that such people are worthy of death. And not just them, but those that have pleasure in such people that commit such sins. Therefore, in essence, the apostle Paul is telling us that all unsaved sinners are worthy of death.

Okay, so, we have just finished Romans, chapter 1, and before we go to chapter 2, I want to offer some more thoughts as to we've just read and seen.

Paul here very clearly outlines the sins of the flesh, the sins of mankind. And if you die in this way of life, you are going to be forever separated from the Lord. But He can change you, He can rescue you, and He can give you a new heart. But, as I've said repeatedly, you have to be born again in order to be saved, in order to be rescued, and in order to be changed.

Please turn to Matthew chapter 15. Scripture with Scripture. Just to avoid any doubt and to prove that the entire Bible is consistent when it comes to the sins of man, the sins of the flesh, we've seen what the apostle Paul said about these sins, but what does the Lord Jesus Christ say about these sins? Look at Matthew 15, verse 19: **"For out of the heart proceed evil thoughts, murders, adulteries, fornications, thefts, false witness, blasphemies"**.

Look at verse 18: **"But those things which proceed out of the mouth come forth from the heart; and they defile the man."** Look at verse 20: **"These are *the things* which defile a man: but to eat with unwashen hands defileth not a man."**

The Lord Jesus Christ said these are evil thoughts. Murders: hating someone is murder. Adultery: lusting after someone is adultery. Fornications: premarital sex is fornication and God hates it. Thefts, stealing, false witness, lying, being deceitful, and blasphemies, taking His name in vain. He says it's evil and He condemns it. And this word for fornications or fornication is *porneia*; it's the Greek word for pornography, which covers everything: all illicit sins of the flesh: paedophilia, homosexuality, bestiality, everything. And the Lord says it's evil, it's wicked.

And I will give you one more Scripture and then I will conclude this broadcast.

Please turn to Revelation 21. Again, Scripture with Scripture. We've seen the apostle Paul on this subject, we've seen the Lord Jesus on this subject. What does the apostle John say about this subject? Revelation, please, 21 and look at verse 8: **"But the fearful, and unbelieving, and the abominable, and murderers, and whoremongers, and sorcerers, and idolaters, and all liars, shall have their part in the lake which burneth with fire and brimstone: which is the second death."** Sorcery, clairvoyants, mediums, praying to dead people. The Bible says it's wicked and if you don't repent of it, into the lake of fire you go, which is the second death, which lasts forever. Liars, idolaters, whoremongers, people that sleep around, the fearful, and the unbelieving are all abominable in the eyes of the Lord. If you're found in here, Revelation 21, or if you are found in Romans chapter 1, or if you are found in Matthew 15, you are in trouble. You need to repent, and you need a Saviour to save you from your sins.

So, as we were concluding from chapter 1, I gave you a very quick footnote, really, with some additional information about how the Lord sees sin and what He's going to do with sin. And part of Romans chapter 1 was not only man's rejection of the Lord Jesus Christ, but how it was foretold that mankind would not only reject the Lord Jesus Christ, but how he would also hate the Lord Jesus Christ. You see, man knows who Jesus Christ is. You can go anywhere in the world and speak to anyone at any given time about any particular subject and, for the most part, it doesn't cause any controversy. But, the moment you mention the Lord Jesus Christ, everything changes.

Please turn to the Book of Isaiah. Isaiah is an Old Testament prophet, and he wrote this book 700 years before the birth of the Lord Jesus Christ. Isaiah 52, look at verse 13: **"Behold, my servant shall deal prudently, he shall be exalted and extolled, and be very high."** A reference to the Lord Jesus Christ written, as I say, 700 years B.C., found in the Old Testament, written by the prophet Isaiah. Look at verse 14: **"As many were astonied at thee; his visage was so marred more than any man, and his form more than the sons of men".**

Verse 14 is clearly in reference to the crucifixion. And did you know that the word "crucifixion" was created to try and explain the pain and suffering that the Lord Jesus Christ went through? When people say it was excruciating, please think about the crucifixion of the Lord Jesus Christ. How the God of the universe hung on a cross, naked, for 6 hours. They crucified Him. The Assyrians started this brutal form of capital punishment, but the Romans perfected it to a "T".

Look at verse 15: **"So shall he sprinkle many nations; the kings shall shut their mouths at him: for *that* which had not been told them shall they see; and *that* which they had not heard shall they consider."** Verses 13 and 14 is primarily in reference to the First Coming; verse 15 is in reference to the Second Coming. More on that in another video.

Please turn to chapter 53. Scripture with Scripture. We are still in the Book of Isaiah. And like I say, mankind doesn't only reject the Lord Jesus Christ. Mankind perpetually hates the Lord Jesus Christ. When you watch television, you hear, "Oh my..." and they say, "God" or "Jesus", and they say "Christ". That's blasphemy. I've been all over the world, and I've heard people blaspheme God. Isn't that amazing? Foretold 700 years B.C., and prophecy is being fulfilled every single day of the week. Hollywood is guilty of it. All of the media around the world are guilty of it, and the U.K. is no exception, I might add.

Isaiah 53. Look at verse 3: **"He is despised and rejected of men; a man of sorrows, and acquainted with grief: and we hid as it were *our* faces from him; he was despised, and we esteemed him not."** In reference primarily to the apostles' running away at the cross, only the women stayed faithful to Him. But that part in verse 3 which says, **"He is despised".** Present tense! **"and rejected of men".** Everybody before they were saved rejected Him, despised Him. Foretold, one more time, 700 years B.C.: **"a man of sorrows, and acquainted with grief".** He bore the sins of the world on His body.

Look at verse 6: **"All we like sheep have gone astray; we have turned every one to his own way; and the LORD hath laid** on him the iniquity of us all." Everyone has sinned. We've all sinned and fallen short of the glory of God. Look at verse 10: **"Yet it pleased the LORD to bruise him; he hath put _him_ to grief: when thou shalt make his soul an offering for sin, he shall see _his_ seed, he shall prolong _his_ days, and the pleasure of the LORD shall prosper in his hand."** Verse 10 makes it very clear that the Lord God, Elohim, was pleased to bruise Him.

Please turn to Genesis chapter 3. One more Scripture to explain this theme of mine and prophecy found in Scripture concerning the man Christ Jesus.

Genesis chapter 3, look at verse 15: **"And I will put enmity between thee and the woman, and between thy seed and her seed; it shall bruise thy head, and thou shalt bruise his heel."** In reference to Satan and the Messiah, of course. Foretold thousands of years before His arrival on the earth, and yet we see from Isaiah 53 how it pleased the Lord to bruise Him, the Lord Jesus Christ. And finally, He made His soul an offering for sin. Incredible! So, put all these Scriptures together and you find a Man sent to earth from eternity past to die for the sins of the world, a Man that was despised and rejected of men. Go anywhere in the world, speak to anyone about any particular person, and for the most part it's going to be okay. But mention the Lord Jesus Christ and everything changes. Why? Because men love darkness rather than light. It's a heart problem, not a head problem. But next up, we'll look at chapter 2 from the Book of Romans.

# CHAPTER 2



**V**ERSE 1: "Therefore thou art inexcusable, O man, whosoever thou art that judgest: for wherein thou judgest another, thou condemnest thyself; for thou that judgest doest the same things."

Chapter 2, verse 1, is a fulfilment of chapter 1, verse 32, where the Lord makes it very clear that unsaved people that have rejected Him, not only continue in their rebellion against Him, but they know that judgment is coming as well. Now Paul says in chapter 2, verse 1, you are inexcusable, oh man, because you judge someone else for the same sins that you are committing yourself. The Lord Jesus Christ says in Matthew chapter 7, **"Judge not, that ye be not judged"**, meaning don't rebuke somebody else or don't judge somebody else for a particular sin if you are committing the same sin yourself. That is hypocrisy and the Lord hates it.

**VERSES 2-3: "But we are sure that the judgment of God is according to truth against them which commit such things. And thinkest thou this, O man, that judgest them which do such things, and doest the same, that thou shalt escape the judgment of God?"**

Of course not. If you are judging person A for committing this sin or that sin, and you are doing it yourself, you have also just condemned yourself. Because by condemning somebody else for the same sin that you are committing, you realise that it is sinful and you have just clearly judged yourself. So, if you are going to judge another party for whatever sin it may be, make sure you are not practising the same sin yourself.

This hypocrisy is found very clearly in the gospels, and in John chapter 8, the Pharisees discovered a woman caught in the act of adultery and they brought her unto the Lord, wanting His permission to stone her. And the Lord Jesus Christ **"stooped down and, with *his* finger, wrote on the ground, *as though he heard them not"*,** found in verse 6. These self-righteous Pharisees were baying for blood, and yes, the Mosaic Law called for death to anyone caught in the act of adultery, bestiality, fornication, homosexuality, and other sins of the flesh. And some commentators over the years have suggested that He has just written their names in the sand and next to their names, the sins that they too were guilty of. And no doubt, adultery was one of them. **"He that is without sin among you, let him first cast a stone at her."** There isn't a just man on the face of the earth.

Look at verse 9: **"And they which heard *it*, being convicted by *their own* conscience, went out one by one, beginning at the eldest, *even* unto the last: and Jesus was left alone, and the woman standing in the midst."**

Go back to Romans, chapter 2, please. So, the Scripture does uphold judgment, but not hypocritical judgment. Righteous, holy, and non-hypocritical judgment. A saved person, therefore, can most certainly judge an unsaved person, but only if they are free from that particular sin that they are judging.

So, moving on through chapter 2 of the Epistle to the Romans, and we saw very clearly from verses 1, 2 and 3, how those that condemn others have just condemned themselves, because they are guilty of the same sin that they are judging others of. And the Lord condemned that from Matthew chapter 7. And here Paul is simply reaffirming the Lord Jesus' teachings on this subject. Don't be a hypocrite when it comes to judging somebody else. Put your own house in order first before you judge someone else.

So, let's start today's broadcast in verse 4: **"Or despisest thou the riches of his goodness and forbearance and longsuffering; not knowing that the goodness of God leadeth thee to repentance?"**

I've been a Bible-believing Christian for 11 years now, and before I got saved, I could have died on many different occasions due to stupid things that I did in my youth, and I was a hypocrite. I was a sinner of all sinners, and I could so easily have died and gone to Hell due to my sins. And Paul says here, Don't you know and why do you despise the goodness of God's longsuffering and His forbearance? Don't you know that the Lord is longsuffering and His patience allows you to be saved?

He waited for many years until I got saved. His longsuffering completely transformed my life. I should have died many times over, like I say, and I deserved to go to Hell for all of my sins. But praise be to God! He saved me, and His goodness and His forbearance and His longsuffering resulted in this sinner getting saved over 11 years ago.

Paul is really slamming the self-righteous Pharisee, the so-called super-duper Christian, the "holier-than-thou" character. The type of person who can always see errors and flaws in other people, but when it comes to himself, he thinks he is perfect. He thinks he is so self-righteous. Like the Pharisees found back in the gospels. The reverent fathers. The scholars. The brains. And Jesus condemned those people as serpents and vipers, and full of iniquity and hypocrisy.

So, if you are still living and breathing and existing on this earth, maybe the Lord has a plan for you, maybe He still wants you to be saved. But you have to come to Him in order to be saved. He won't reveal Himself to you if there is sin in your life. But if you want to be saved, get on your knees and call on His name. Because it is His will for you to be saved.

So, moving on through the Epistle to the Romans, and we are very much still in chapter 2. And we read from the previous broadcast how the Lord's goodness and forbearance and longsuffering does lead sinners to repentance. It worked for me, and it can work for you if you call on the name of the Lord Jesus Christ.

But let's start today's broadcast, if we may, in verses 5-11: **"But after thy hardness and impenitent heart treasurest up unto thyself wrath against the day of wrath and revelation of the righteous judgment of God; Who will render to every man according to his deeds: To them who by patient continuance in well doing seek for glory and honour and immortality, eternal life: But unto them that are contentious, and do not obey the truth, but obey**

**unrighteousness, indignation and wrath, Tribulation and anguish, upon every soul of man that doeth evil, of the Jew first, and also of the Gentile; But glory, honour, and peace, to every man that worketh good, to the Jew first, and also to the Gentile: For there is no respect of persons with God."**

Verse 11 should be underlined in your Bible. There is no respect of persons with the Lord. You are either saved or you are not saved. He judged His own people due to their sin. Moses, Miriam and Aaron did not go into the Promised Land due to their sin. He still loved them, but due to their sin, they did not go into the Promised Land.

You cannot bribe the Lord. If there is sin in your life and you don't deal with it, He will deal with you. So, for those that continue on in their sin, found also back in chapter 1, from verses 18 down to 32, and here reaffirmed from verses 5 down to 10, you will get yours. You may enjoy your sin for a while. You may be very popular with your peers. But one day you will die and you will stand in the presence of Almighty God, and He will judge you according to what the Bible says. If you've lied, you are a liar. If you've stolen, you are a thief. If you've lusted after a woman, you are an adulterer. And if you have hated somebody, the Bible says you are a murderer. He will judge your heart and He will judge your thought life. Never mind your works; they get judged too. But He will judge your heart and He will judge your thought life as well. As a man thinks in his heart, so is he.

And at the same time, He also holds out the hand of friendship and fellowship to those that continue on in well-doing, who seek glory and honour, immortality, eternal life, that obey the truth and love righteousness. But verse 9 says, **"Tribulation and anguish, upon every soul of man that doeth evil, of the Jew first, and also of the Gentile".** You can't escape the judgment of God. If you die without Jesus Christ, you will go to Hell for all of eternity, pure and simple. But that's not His will for you.

So, we are still in the Epistle to the Romans, chapter 2, and we aren't even halfway through this magnificent masterpiece of the apostle Paul. If you are saved, this epistle should be of great comfort to you. But if you are not saved, this epistle is very much against you. You are either for the Lord or you are against the Lord. There is no middle ground.

But let's start today's broadcast, if we may, in verses 12-16: **"For as many as have sinned without law shall also perish without law: and as many as have sinned in the law shall be judged by the law; (For not the hearers of the law *are* just before God, but the doers of the law shall be justified. For when the Gentiles, which have not the law, do by nature the things contained in the law, these, having not the law, are a law unto themselves: Which shew the work of the law written in their hearts, their conscience also bearing witness, and *their* thoughts the mean while accusing or else excusing one another;) In the day when God shall judge the secrets of men by Jesus Christ according to my gospel."**

Chapter 1, he says, **"my God".** Chapter 2, he says, **"my gospel".** But, go back to verse 12, please. There are many people that are sinning outside of the law, the law being the Ten

Commandments, of course. And those people are going to perish outside of the law. The law points you to the Lord Jesus Christ, the law shows you that you are a sinner, in need of a Saviour. If you take the law away from mankind, you cause chaos and mayhem. Yes, they have a conscience which convicts them when they sin, found in verse 15, but the law nevertheless, came from the Lord to point mankind to Him.

Also, from verse 12, the apostle Paul says, **"as many as have sinned in the law shall be judged by the law"**, meaning the Jews, of course. Never forget that the Ten Commandments were given primarily to the children of Israel, not the Gentile nations. But they are still going to be judged by the standards of the Lord, not the standards of the land.

Verse 13, Paul says, **"For not the hearers of the law *are* just before God, but the doers of the law shall be justified",** and some people say, "Well, you have to keep the law in order to be saved." Please turn to chapter 3, look at verse 28: **"Therefore we conclude that a man is justified by faith without the deeds of the law."** Faith alone. You saw it in chapter 1, verse 16: **"it is the power of God unto salvation to every one that believeth; to the Jew first, and also to the Greek."** Faith alone. Believing. **"The just shall live by faith."**

So, what does it mean to be a doer of the law? Please turn to Matthew chapter 22. Again, Scripture with Scripture. Matthew 22. Look at verse 37, please. **"Jesus said unto him, Thou shalt love the Lord thy God with all thy heart, and with all thy soul, and with all thy mind. This is the first and great commandment. And the second *is* like unto it,**

**Thou shalt love thy neighbour as thyself. On these two commandments hang all the law and the prophets."** To love the Lord your God with all your mind, with all your heart and with all your soul comes after you have been born again. And once you love the Lord your God with all your mind, heart, soul and strength, you are then expected to love your neighbour as yourself.

Please turn to Romans chapter 13. Look at verse 8: **"Owe no man any thing, but to love one another: for he that loveth another hath fulfilled the law."** Love the Lord thy God, love thy neighbour as thyself means that you have kept and fulfilled the law. But keeping the Ten Commandments does not save you. Once you are saved and you walk in the Spirit, you can do anything. But Jesus has enabled you to do those things because you are born again, not in order to be born again, but because you are already born again.

So, during the last broadcast, we looked at verses 12 down to 16, and Paul says, **"In the day when God shall judge the secrets of men by Jesus Christ, according to my gospel."** That day found in verse 16 is the Great White Throne. And if you die without the Lord Jesus Christ, He, the Lord Jesus, is going to judge you at the Great White Throne Judgment. You won't escape His judgment. He will judge your heart, and He will judge your thoughts, and He will also judge your deeds. But, at the same time, we saw, from cross-references, how keeping the law does not save us.

In verse 14, the apostle Paul says, **"For when the Gentiles, which have not the law, do by nature the things contained**

**in the law"**, like stealing, like murdering, like committing fornication or adultery. The Ten Commandments were given to the Jews, and apart from the Sabbath, which has no direct reference to us, the Gentiles, the rest of the Ten Commandments are still applicable. God will judge you by the Ten Commandments, whether you are Jew or Gentile, it is immaterial. He will still judge you the same way. And Paul says, these Gentiles are a law unto themselves. How true that is. If you were to go back to the 1930s and look at Nazi Germany, you would have seen all sorts of laws being introduced which were abhorrent. They were wicked, they were evil.

These Gentiles were a law unto themselves. They tried to create their own morality. They passed laws which made it legal to kill Jews and gypsies and Christians and anyone who opposed what they stood for. And verse 14 really does bring it home to me that these Gentiles which have not the law do by nature the things contained in the law and they become a law unto themselves. How true that it is!

So, verse 14 makes it very clear as to what happens when those that live outside of the law and yet are doing the things in the law become a law unto themselves. We saw it back in the 1930s and 1940s in Nazi Germany, and we saw it back in the Soviet Union, under the Communist regime. They passed laws as well. They did tests on their own people which were ruthless. Why? Because they were unsaved Gentiles, doing things which were contained in the law, and once again, they became a law unto themselves.

And verse 15, Paul says it very clearly, **"Which shew the work of the law written in their hearts, their conscience also bearing witness, and *their* thoughts the mean while accusing or else excusing one another"**. It goes back to Romans chapter 1, verse 32. These people know what they are doing is wrong, and they know that judgment is coming. And yet they continue on in their sin, totally regardless, totally indifferent.

What more can the Lord God of the Bible do? He's given man a conscience, He's given man a creation, and He's given mankind the Bible. What more can He do?

And one more time from verse 16: **"In the day when God shall judge the secrets of men by Jesus Christ according to my gospel"**. Every thought, every deed, every action He has seen, He has noted, and He is going to judge you for it unless you repent now and believe on His Son. Otherwise, you will stand completely naked at the Great White Throne and He will judge you like a forensic lawyer would do, and He will go through every aspect of your life in fine detail. So, choose you this day what you are going to do. Are you going to bend the knee and believe on the Lord Jesus Christ, or you going to snub Him and embrace sin even more? The ball, therefore, is very much in your court.

So, we are nearing the end of chapter 2 of the Epistle to the Romans. And during the last broadcast, we saw very clearly as to what happens when man turns from the Lord and creates his own truth, when he creates his own reality and the consequences are always deadly for those that are living under such systems. And like I said last time, even if we had no Bibles, we still have a conscience which comes from Heaven and we have a creation which always points back to a Creator. So, mankind, according to verse 16, is without excuse. It's as simple as that.

Look at verses 17-20: **"Behold, thou art called a Jew, and restest in the law, and makest thy boast of God, And knowest *his* will, and approvest the things that are more excellent, being instructed out of the law; And art confident that thou thyself art a guide of the blind, a light of them which are in darkness, An instructor of the foolish, a teacher of babes, which hast the form of knowledge and of the truth in the law."**

Paul has gone from focusing on atheists and agnostics, and all non-theists to some extent, and now he is going to focus his attention on the Jews. Because Paul was a Jew. Paul was a Jew of the Jews. He was a Pharisee of the Pharisees; he was a scholar of the scholars. And here he's going to zoom in to the average Jewish man or woman who's trusting ultimately in his knowledge of the law, and not in the finished work of the Lord Jesus Christ on the cross.

Look at verses 21-22, please: **"Thou therefore which teachest another, teachest thou not thyself? thou that preachest a man should not steal, dost thou steal? Thou that sayest a man should not commit adultery, dost thou commit adultery? thou that abhorrest idols, dost thou commit sacrilege?"**

It goes back to Matthew, chapter 7. Don't judge somebody for doing the same thing that you are doing. This is common sense; this is primitive teaching. And yet Paul has to say it, because the Pharisees were the masters of being holier than thou. Hypocrites with a capital "H". And God said, 'you people are worthy of hellfire, because you aren't saved and you are preaching this self-righteous message, which nobody can keep. Only My Son kept the law perfectly and, therefore, you are going to Hell and your disciples and your converts are going to Hell as well.'

In verse 21 he says, you therefore which teach another, do you not teach yourself? Do as I say, not as I do? These people say, "Don't steal", but are they stealing? They go on to say, "Don't commit adultery," but are they committing adultery? Go back to John chapter 8 and read it again. Verse 22 also says they oppose idols, and yet Paul says, **"Do you commit sacrilege?"** An idol can be absolutely anything. Your mind can be an idol, which feeds back into verse 20: **"An instructor of the foolish, a teacher of babes, which hast the form of knowledge and of the truth in the law."** They loved to learn, they loved knowledge, they loved to speak, they loved to debate. They are always learning, but never able to come to the knowledge of the truth.

So, we have finally arrived at the end of chapter 2. And thank you for bearing with me. This epistle is very deep and it's very rich, and it's very unapologetic as well. Like I say, if you're for the Lord, this epistle should give you great comfort, but if you are against the Lord, this epistle is very much against you.

Let's conclude this broadcast and this chapter in verses 23-29: **"Thou that makest thy boast of the law, through breaking the law dishonourest thou God? For the name of God is blasphemed among the Gentiles through you, as it is written. For circumcision verily profiteth, if thou keep the law: but if thou be a breaker of the law, thy circumcision is made uncircumcision. Therefore if the uncircumcision keep the righteousness of the law, shall not his uncircumcision be counted for circumcision? And shall not uncircumcision which is by nature, if it fulfil the law, judge thee, who by the letter and circumcision dost transgress the law? For he is not a Jew, which is one outwardly; neither *is that* circumcision, which is outward in the flesh: But he *is* a Jew, which is one inwardly; and circumcision *is that* of the heart, in the spirit, *and* not in the letter; whose praise *is* not of men, but of God."**

Verse 24 is very interesting, because Paul says how the name of God is blasphemed by the Gentiles when they see hypocritical, self-righteous Jews living after the flesh, saying one thing but doing another. And again, God is very much against that. This whole theme of circumcision, in a nutshell, means nothing. For those living under the New Covenant, it doesn't make any difference if you are circumcised or not. Your heart is the issue, not your body *per se*. And of course, when I refer to your heart, I don't mean your literal heart, but your spiritual heart, which has been born again. You got a new heart when you were born again.

And verse 17 also ties in quite nicely with verses 23 down to 29. These were Jews which were also resting in the law and offering some kind of outward worship to the Lord. But their hearts were dead. They were like the Pharisees, they were far from the one true God. They gave Him lip service. They may have been Jews. They may have been circumcised. They may even have been teachers, but unless their hearts were circumcised, they were just as lost as a typical Gentile. And verse 29, one more time, to conclude chapter 2: "But he *is* a Jew, which is one inwardly; and circumcision *is that* of the heart, in the spirit, *and* not in the letter; whose praise *is* not of men, but of God." He loves God, not man. His heart, as I say, has been spiritually circumcised and now he is a true Jew. He is now a true man or woman of God. If you are a Gentile Bible-believing Christian, you are a spiritual Jew. But one more time, it's a heart issue, not a head issue.

# CHAPTER 3

———

**V**ERSE 1: **"What advantage then hath the Jew? or what profit is there of circumcision?"**

Paul starts chapter 3, verse 1, asking the almost rhetorical question: Is there any point in being a Jew? Is there any point in being circumcised? He made it very clear from chapter 2, verses 27, 28 and 29, that only a person whose heart has been circumcised is qualified to be called a Jew. Physical circumcision was all very well, but if the heart of the Jew was not circumcised, it was pointless to be circumcised.

Look at verse 2: **"Much every way: chiefly, because that unto them were committed the oracles of God."**

The Old Testament: the Jews were chosen to be God's people. They were chosen to represent Him; they were chosen to be His vehicle, to bring the Gentiles unto Him. Please turn to the Book of Esther. Please look at chapter 8, verse 15: **"And Mordecai went out from the presence of the king in royal apparel of blue and white, and with a great crown of gold, and with a garment of fine linen and purple: and the city of Shushan rejoiced and was glad."** Mordecai was a Jew and here the Gentiles from the city of Shushan are rejoicing and are glad at Mordecai who's been elevated in the kingdom of the Gentiles, but more specific, the people of Persia.

Look at verse 16: **"The Jews had light, and gladness, and joy, and honour. And in every province, and in every city, whithersoever the king's commandment and his decree came, the Jews had joy and gladness, a feast and a good day. And many of the people of the land became Jews; for the fear of the Jews fell upon them."** The Church should be able to do this. These pagan Gentiles became Jews due to the testimony of the Jewish people, who experienced gladness, joy and honour. The Jews were chosen by the Lord to be a vehicle to the Gentiles, but they failed on a mass scale.

Please turn to Deuteronomy, chapter 7. God's love for the Jews is unconditional and, although they rejected the Lord Jesus Christ and, in fact, they rejected most of the Old Testament prophets, nevertheless, for the sake of their fathers, the Lord still loves Israel. It makes no difference whether a Jew is walking with the Lord or not, they are still the apple of His eye. But, for now, we the Church are the true people of God. The Jews fell, according to Romans, chapter 11, through unbelief. And during this dispensation of the New Covenant, we the Gentiles, we the Church people, have been grafted in to represent the Lord God of the Bible.

Look at chapter 7, verse 7: **"The LORD did not set his love upon you, nor choose you, because ye were more in number than any people; for ye *were* the fewest of all people: But because the LORD loved you, and because he would keep the oath which he had sworn unto your fathers, hath the LORD brought you out with a mighty hand, and redeemed you out of the house of bondmen, from the hand of Pharaoh king of Egypt."** So, we see very clearly from chapter

7, verse 7, how the Lord chose Israel, which were the least of all the nations, to become His people. And from them came kings, and from all of the kings came the King of Kings, the Lord Jesus Christ.

So, last time, we saw Paul tried to deal with the question that the Jews would have been asking him, Is there any point in being a Jew anymore? Is there any point in being circumcised? And I showed you some references from the Old Testament as to how the Lord dealt with Israel and why He chose Israel to be His people. And we also saw from the Book of Esther how the Jews were able to bring the Gentiles to God through their testimony.

Look at verses 3-4, please: **"For what if some did not believe? shall their unbelief make the faith of God without effect? God forbid: yea, let God be true, but every man a liar; as it is written, That thou mightest be justified in thy sayings, and mightest overcome when thou art judged."**

Paul has to deal with the reality that the people of Israel, for the most part, did not receive the Lord Jesus Christ. And, in fact, they put Him to death. This, of course, was foretold in the Old Testament: the Scriptures found in verse 2, the oracle of God. In fact, the Jews put most of their prophets to death and didn't believe in what they told them. So, when Jesus Christ came, it wasn't any surprise that they would also reject Him and crucify Him.

Look at verses 5-8: **"But if our unrighteousness commend the righteousness of God, what shall we say?** *Is* **God** unrighteous who taketh vengeance? (I speak as a man) God forbid: for then how shall God judge the world? For if the truth of God hath more abounded through my lie unto his glory; why yet am I also judged as a sinner? And not *rather*, (as we be slanderously reported, and as some affirm that we say,) Let us do evil, that good may come? whose damnation is just."

Verse 8, first of all. And here, the apostle Paul is condemning those slanderers. And we have it today, those of us that hold to eternal security, we too are accused unfairly of giving people a licence to sin. Because we are saved, because all of our past, present and future sins have been forgiven, that does not allow us to live in sin. That doesn't allow us to rebel against God. And here, Paul is trying to build on the main theme of Romans: how God is holy, and all of mankind, Jew and Gentile, are wicked, are sinful and very much in need of a Saviour. This theme of mankind needing a mediator between man and God is nothing new. It's found throughout the entire Bible.

But look at Job, chapter 9. Job is the oldest book in the Bible. Look at verse 2: **"I know *it is* so of a truth: but how should man be just with God?"** What a brilliant question! How can man be just with God? Answer: He can't, unless somebody steps into the equation and makes him just, that person, of course, being the Lord Jesus Christ. Job is the oldest book in the Bible, written by Moses around 1500 B.C., and Job lived many years even before the patriarchs arrived on the scene. And this question has been asked over the centuries by philosophers and religious people. How should man be just with God? Answer: Jesus Christ.

We saw from verses 1 to 8 how the apostle Paul made it very clear that circumcision and keeping the law weren't really the issues that the Lord was concerned about. He wanted Jews to be circumcised in their hearts, a spiritual circumcision which comes, of course, at the new birth. Until a Jew was circumcised in his heart, he wasn't a true Jew, according to chapter 2, verses 27 to 29. This was a very thorny issue. This was a very painful issue. And once the temple had been destroyed, the Jews went into meltdown. What do we do? What is happening? And you can only hope that those Jews living around 70 A.D. would have read the Epistle to the Romans. It's all in here as to what God would have expected of Jews to do if they wanted to be right with him.

So, let's start today's broadcast in verses 9-18: **"What then? are we better *than* they? No, in no wise: for we have before proved both Jews and Gentiles, that they are all under sin; As it is written, There is none righteous, no, not one: There is none that understandeth, there is none that seeketh after God. They are all gone out of the way, they are together become unprofitable; there is none that doeth good, no, not one. Their throat is an open sepulchre; with their tongues they have used deceit; the poison of asps *is* under their lips: Whose mouth *is* full of cursing and bitterness: Their feet *are* swift to shed blood: Destruction and misery *are* in their ways: And the way of peace have they not known: There is no fear of God before their eyes."**

In verse 9 he says **"we"**, meaning all of the apostles have before proved how all Jews and all Gentiles are all under sin, without exception. He goes on to quote Psalm 14 and Psalm 53, and these verses should be read in conjunction with chapter 1, verses 18 down to 32. When man turns from God, God turns from man. Look at Genesis, chapter 6, when the Lord flooded the earth due to immorality. Look at Genesis, chapter 19, when God destroyed Sodom and Gomorrah with fire. From Genesis, chapter 6, everybody was drowned except one family. From Genesis, chapter 19, everybody in the region of Sodom and Gomorrah was destroyed apart from one man and his two daughters. So from verse 9, down to 18 should be read very carefully. Mankind, in his pre-salvation state, is a wicked, despicable, depraved sinner who is worthy of death according to chapter 1, verse 32. But God sent Jesus to come to earth to die for the sins of the world. **"The Son of man is come to seek and to save that which was lost"** (Luke 19:10).

So, moving through chapter 3 of the Epistle to the Romans, the last time we saw very clearly how Jew or Gentile, male or female – it makes no difference–, all are equally guilty in the eyes of the Lord God of the Bible.

So, let's start today's broadcast in verse 19: **"Now we know that what things soever the law saith, it saith to them who are under the law: that every mouth may be stopped, and all the world may become guilty before God."**

When you stand at the Great White Throne Judgment if you are not saved, your mouth will be stopped. You will be speechless. You will stand in the presence of Almighty God, being in the Person of Jesus Christ, and you will be naked. Every thought, word and deed will be judged. Your sins, which may have been in secret, are now going to be made public. The

Lord God of the Bible is going to judge every thought, word and deed. And He will find you guilty, because nobody made you sin those sins that you committed. And a guilty verdict will send you to the lake of fire for all eternity.

Look at verse 20: **"Therefore by the deeds of the law there shall no flesh be justified in his sight: for by the law *is* the knowledge of sin."**

Chapter 2, verses 12, 13, 14 and 15 made it very clear that universally mankind knows there's a Creator, and his conscience bears record to the Creator of the universe. When he sins, he knows that he has done wrong. So, he is without excuse. But two things in verse 20: **"by the deeds of the law there shall no flesh be justified in his sight"**, meaning if you could keep the Ten Commandments, it wouldn't save you anyway, and by the presence of the law is the knowledge of sin. **"Thou shalt not…" "Thou shalt not…" "Thou shalt not…"** These things all point to Almighty God. He is the judge, He sets the rules, He sets the parameters. And those Ten Commandments point you back to the Lord. Therefore, you are without excuse. Verse 19: that **"all the world may become guilty before God"**. You may have escaped this travesty; you may have been able to keep this sin secret. But one day, everything is going to be brought out into the open.

Okay, so, concluding chapter 3 of the Epistle to the Romans, and last time we saw very clearly and unequivocally, how Jews and Gentiles are not going to escape the judgment of God. It makes no difference whether these people are saved or not. Everybody is going to be judged. For a saved person, they are going to be judged at the Judgment Seat of Christ. And for an unsaved person, they are going to be judged at the Great White Throne Judgment. It makes no difference, like I say, the Lord is no respecter of persons.

Let's start today's broadcast in verses 21-26: **"But now the righteousness of God without the law is manifested, being witnessed by the law and the prophets; Even the righteousness of God *which is* by faith of Jesus Christ unto all and upon all them that believe: for there is no difference: For all have sinned, and come short of the glory of God; Being justified freely by his grace through the redemption that is in Christ Jesus: Whom God hath set forth *to be* a propitiation through faith in his blood, to declare his righteousness for the remission of sins that are past, through the forbearance of God; To declare, *I say*, at this time his righteousness: that he might be just, and the justifier of him which believeth in Jesus."**

From 21 down to 26, the apostle Paul was on a roll. In verse 23, he says: **"For all have sinned, and come short of the glory of God"** and we continue to come short of the glory of God, even if we are saved, I might add.

In verse 24, he says: **"Being justified freely by his grace through the redemption that is in Christ Jesus".** Grace is God's unmerited favour, it's a free gift. **"The just shall live by faith".**

In verse 26, he says **"To declare, *I say*, at this time his righteousness: that he might be just, and the justifier of him**

**which believeth in Jesus."** Once again, you have to believe on the Lord Jesus Christ. True remorse for your sins and real faith in the Lord Jesus Christ as Saviour and Lord. He died on the cross in your place. He was a propitiation for your sins and for my sins.

Just one quick footnote, if I may, from verse 25. Yes, God sent Jesus to be a propitiation for our sins and it pleased God for Him to offer Himself for the sins of the world.

Please turn quickly in your Bibles to Isaiah 53, and I'll close this broadcast in verse 12: **"Therefore will I divide him *a portion* with the great, and he shall divide the spoil with the strong; because he hath poured out his soul unto death: and he was numbered with the transgressors; and he bare the sin of many, and made intercession for the transgressors."** Written 700 years B.C., very much in reference to the death, burial and resurrection of the Lord Jesus Christ. He made a propitiation for the sins of the world, he has made a provision for everybody to be saved. But only those that appropriate the atonement, meaning only those that believe on Him with true and real faith, are going to be saved. All others, therefore, will die in their sins and go to Hell forever. Not God's choice, but that is as a result of the free will of man. Heaven or Hell, the choice is yours. We found it very clearly defined in the latter verses of chapter 3 how God has made it possible to reconcile the world unto Himself.

And in verse 27, the apostle Paul says: **"Where *is* boasting then? It is excluded. By what law? of works? Nay: but by the law of faith."**

Your good works are not going to save you. All of these self-righteous Jews that were keeping the law, that had been circumcised, that had been custodians of the oracles of God are still going to fall short of the glory of God. Gentiles, which are a law until themselves, have also fallen short of the glory of God. The law won't save you and works won't save you.

Look at verse 28: **"Therefore we conclude that a man is justified by faith without the deeds of the law."**

Keeping the Ten Commandments, even if you could, won't save you. Chapter 1, verse 17: **"The just shall live by faith".**

Chapter 3, verse 20: **"Therefore by the deeds of the law there shall no flesh be justified in his sight".**

Chapter 3, verse 24: **"Being justified freely by his grace through the redemption that is in Christ Jesus".** It couldn't be any clearer. But some people fail to understand this, and they add wicked works to the finished work of the Lord Jesus Christ. Once you are saved, you can do good works. And the Epistle to the Ephesians, chapter 2, says we have been saved unto good works. The works come after we are saved. But the works in and of themselves don't save us. Pure and simple!

**VERSES 29-30: *"Is he* the God of the Jews only? *is he* not also of the Gentiles? Yes, of the Gentiles also: Seeing *it is* one God, which shall justify the circumcision by faith, and uncircumcision through faith."**

Two points from verse 30: those Jews that have been physically circumcised and had gone on to believe on the Lord Jesus

Christ, like Peter, Paul and John, and Andrew and James, and all of the other apostles, were saved by their faith. Period! And those Gentiles that were not circumcised and are not going to be circumcised, but have true faith in the Lord Jesus Christ, they too will be saved by faith in the Messiah. One more time, **"The just shall live by faith".**

**VERSE 31: "Do we then make void the law through faith? God forbid: yea, we establish the law."**

When we walk in the spirit, we establish, we fulfil the law.

# CHAPTER 4

VERSE 1: "What shall we say then that Abraham our father, as pertaining to the flesh, hath found?"

I'm going to call chapter 4, "The Faith Chapter". *Sola Fide.* We saw very clearly from chapter 3, verse 20, how by the deeds of the law no flesh will be justified in His sight, and we saw very clearly from verse 28 how a man is justified by faith without the deeds of the law. And here the apostle Paul is going to go back to the Old Testament and look at how Abraham, the father of all nations, got saved. And we also discovered from chapter 2, verse 27 down to 29, how the Lord expected more than just a head knowledge of Him.

Being a Jew through circumcision, going to the synagogue, or going to the temple, as they did back in here, 56 A.D., was all very well, but Jesus said back in John, chapter 4, that a time was coming when those that wanted to worship the Lord would have to do so in truth and in spirit.

Being an outward Jew wouldn't saved you; it never did save you. Being a Jew, keeping the rituals, going to the temple, so and so forth, showed you that you needed to be saved. For the Scripture said, **"for by the law *is* the knowledge of sin"** (Romans 3:20).

Look at verse 2: **"For if Abraham were justified by works, he hath *whereof* to glory; but not before God."**

If works could save you, Abraham would win, hands down. He was called when he was 75 years old to follow the Lord. By the time he made 100, Isaac was born. He believed on the Lord that he would have a son, and from his son, many nations would be blessed.

**VERSE 3: "For what saith the scripture? Abraham believed God, and it was counted unto him for righteousness."**

The Scripture, the oracles of God, the Jewish Tenach. Please turn to Genesis 15. Scripture with Scripture. Let's start in verse 4: **"And, behold, the word of the LORD *came* unto him, saying, This shall not be thine heir; but he that shall come forth out of thine own bowels shall be thine heir. 5 And he brought him forth abroad, and said, Look now toward heaven, and tell the stars, if thou be able to number them: and he said unto him, So shall thy seed be."** Look at verse 6: **"And he believed in the LORD; and he counted it to him for righteousness."** The just shall live by faith. God says to Abraham, do you believe that from Isaac your seed shall be blessed? And Abraham says, yes, Lord. I believe. And the Lord said, fine, you are now saved.

Look at chapter 12, please, verses 1-3: **"Now the LORD had said unto Abram, Get thee out of thy country, and from thy kindred, and from thy father's house, unto a land that I will shew thee: And I will make of thee a great nation, and I will bless thee, and make thy name great; and thou shalt be a blessing: And I will bless them that bless thee, and curse him that curseth thee: and in thee shall all families of the earth be blessed."**

One more Scripture: please turn to chapter 17 of Genesis. Look at verse 23: **"And Abraham took Ishmael his son, and all that were born in his house, and all that were bought with his money, every male among the men of Abraham's house; and circumcised the flesh of their foreskin in the selfsame day, as God had said unto him."**

In Genesis chapter 12, Abraham was called. In Genesis chapter 15, Abraham believed on the Lord and got saved. In Genesis 17, he circumcised all of the men in his house. Now if you want to spiritualise that to somebody living today, this is how you could do it: Genesis, chapter 12, the Lord called man to believe on Him, which would be a general call to repentance. Genesis, chapter 15, the Lord says to the sinner, do you believe on my Son as your Saviour? And the sinner says yes, and the Lord says, you are now saved. And by Genesis chapter 17, the saved sinner has now got baptised. And all of his house, if they are also of age and have also believed on the Lord, get baptised as well. But ultimately, what is important is how that person got saved: faith in the one true God. *Sola Fide*. Faith alone.

So, during the last broadcast, we looked at Genesis 12, 15 and 17. And we saw how Abraham got saved. Paul is building on his case how sinners have always been saved the same way, through faith alone. Chapter 3, verses 20 and 28, made it very clear from the Book of Romans how a man is justified, meaning exonerated, by faith without the deeds of the law.

Please turn to Philippians chapter 3. Let's start in verse 7: **"But what things were gain to me, those I counted loss for Christ. Yea doubtless, and I count all things *but* loss for the** excellency of the knowledge of Christ Jesus my Lord: for whom I have suffered the loss of all things, and do count them *but* dung, that I may win Christ. And be found in him, not having mine own righteousness, which is of the law, but that which is through the faith of Christ, the righteousness which is of God by faith: That I may know him, and the power of his resurrection, and the fellowship of his sufferings, being made conformable unto his death; If by any means I might attain unto the resurrection of the dead." Paul was a Jew of the Jews, and here he makes it very clear how he was prepared to lose everything in order to win Christ Jesus, to be conformable unto His death. And he says in verse 9, **"And be found in him, not having mine own righteousness,"** meaning my good works, my Jewish rituals, my circumcision, my good works, this and that. No! **"But that which is through the faith of Christ, the righteousness which is of God by faith."** One more time: **"the just shall live by faith".**

Verse 10 and 11, he speaks about wanting to know the power of the resurrection and to be identified with the fellowship and the sufferings of the Saviour. That's glorification. When a man gets saved he is justified, which means he has been exonerated from all of his past, present and future sins. Once that happens, the Lord sanctifies you, which means he puts you apart. We saw that word in chapter 1, verse 1. But sanctification is also an ongoing process, where the Lord grows you from within, and He matures you. And here Paul, saved about 35 years, hasn't quite made it to perfection. And you won't make it to perfection in this lifetime either, I might add.

Look at verse 12, please: **"Not as though I had already attained, either were already perfect: but I follow after, if that I may apprehend that for which also I am apprehended of Christ Jesus."** That's glorification. That comes after a man dies. When a person gets saved, they are positionally perfect in the eyes of the Lord, but their daily standing with the Lord can and does fluctuate, found very clearly here in verse 12. He wasn't yet perfect. And neither are you and neither am I. But he got saved by believing on the Lord Jesus Christ, without the deeds of the law, not having his own righteousness, but that which comes through the faith of Christ, the righteousness which is of God by faith.

Please go back to Romans, chapter 4. So, we are still very much in the early verses of chapter 4. Paul made it very clear how a man got saved, and it wasn't by keeping the law or being a good person. The Lord Jesus said nobody is good but God. Abraham, the great patriarch, believed on the Lord and God saved him. And I showed you from Philippians chapter 3, how the apostle Paul got saved. A Jew of the Jews, but he knew it could not save him. And like a beggar, he reached out to the Saviour and said, Lord, please save a wretched sinner like myself. God, be merciful to me, a sinner! It's not rocket science; it's elementary. But the self-righteous Jews living around this time were very hostile to this teaching; hence why most of the New Testament deals with this theme time after time. And we also discovered very clearly from reading Genesis 12, 15 and 17 how Abraham got saved before he was circumcised. He got saved before he offered up Isaac as a sacrifice to the Lord. Justification in the eyes of the Lord and justification in the eyes of men are two very different things, and I will show you how that works very shortly.

But, for today's broadcast, please, let's start in verse 4: **"Now to him that worketh is the reward not reckoned of grace, but of debt"**,

Meaning God would owe you salvation. The Lord would be in debt to give you salvation. That's not what the Bible teaches. Salvation is a free gift.

**VERSE 5: "But to him that worketh not, but believeth on him that justifieth the ungodly, his faith is counted for righteousness"**,

As was Abraham's. Verses 1 through to 5 he has shown how Abraham got saved without doing anything. Now, he's going to focus on King David, the greatest king in the Old Testament.

Look at verses 6-7: **"Even as David also describeth the blessedness of the man, unto whom God imputeth righteousness without works, *Saying*, Blessed *are* they whose iniquities are forgiven, and whose sins are covered."**

David believed on the Lord and got saved the same way that Abraham believed on the Lord and got saved. Two different men, two different dispensations, two different ministries, but they both got saved the same way. Lord, be merciful to me, a sinner.

Look at verses 8-9a: **"Blessed *is* the man to whom the Lord will not impute sin. *Cometh* this blessedness then upon the circumcision *only*, or upon the uncircumcision also?"**

From verse 8, Paul says the man whom the Lord will not impute sin is blessed, he's happy, he's fortunate.

Please turn to 2 Corinthians, one more time, please, and I will conclude this broadcast in 2 Corinthians. Look at chapter 5, verse 19: **"To wit, that God was in Christ, reconciling the world unto himself, not imputing their trespasses unto them; and hath committed unto us the word of reconciliation."**

Look at chapter 6, verse 2, please: **"behold, now *is* the accepted time; behold, now *is* the day of salvation."** God has reconciled the world unto Himself. **"Be ye reconciled unto Him. Behold, now is the day of salvation."** The Jews kept the law, or so they thought, and yet it could not save them. Jesus Christ came to earth and He has fulfilled the law. **"The Son of Man has come to seek and to save that which was lost"** (Luke 19:10). So, if you want to be saved, get on your knees and say, Lord, be merciful to me, a sinner. And He will save you and He will keep you saved. All the glory goes to the Lord, not mankind. Your works cannot save you; it's all of Him. Faith in Christ alone!

Continuing on through verse 9b: **"for we say that faith was reckoned to Abraham for righteousness."**

We, being the apostles, teach and uphold that Abraham was saved before he was circumcised.

Look at verse 10: **"How was it then reckoned? when he was in circumcision, or in uncircumcision? Not in circumcision, but in uncircumcision."**

Why? Because if he was saved when he was circumcised, that would be considered a work. And verse 4 condemns man being saved by works. Salvation is not a work; salvation is a gift.

Look at verses 11-12, please: **"And he received the sign of circumcision, a seal of the righteousness of the faith which *he had yet* being uncircumcised: that he might be the father of all them that believe, though they be not circumcised; that righteousness might be imputed unto them also: And the father of circumcision to them who are not of the circumcision only, but who also walk in the steps of that faith of our father Abraham, which *he had* being *yet* uncircumcised."**

Verses 9 down through 12 are very clear: Abraham was justified before he was circumcised. Period! And I gave the analogy during a previous broadcast how Genesis 12 showed Abraham being called unto salvation, which would be repentance for today, if you will, and Genesis, chapter 15, how Abraham believed on the Lord and it was counted to Him for righteousness, which today would be the equivalent of a saved sinner repenting. And by Genesis, chapter 17, Abraham and all of his believing house are then circumcised. Circumcision, therefore, could be considered the equivalent of baptism in the New Covenant but please remember this, that circumcision in the Old Testament was only for the men, whereas in the New Testament, men and women need to be baptised once they are saved. But baptism does not save you and I'll show you why.

Please turn to Galatians, chapter 3. Look at verse 1: **"O foolish Galatians, who hath bewitched you, that ye should not obey** the truth, before whose eyes Jesus Christ hath been **evidently set forth, crucified among you? This only would I learn of you, Received ye the Spirit by the works of the law, or by the hearing of faith?"** A very simple question: Did you get saved by fulfilling the deeds of the law, condemned in Romans chapter 3? Or were you saved by the hearing of faith; **"faith cometh by hearing, and hearing by the word of God"** (Romans 10:17).

See verse 3: **"Are ye so foolish? having begun in the Spirit, are ye now made perfect by the flesh?"** And verses 4, 5, 6 and 7 make it very clear how Abraham was saved by faith. The Galatians were saved by faith. The Romans were saved by faith. I was saved by faith, and you got saved by faith, if you are born again. Chapter 3, verse 1: **"O foolish Galatians, who hath bewitched you...?"** A stinging indictment by the apostle Paul. These people were Gentiles. They got saved by grace through faith in Christ alone, and yet for some bizarre reason, they tried to better themselves by keeping the law. And Paul says it one more time in verse 2: **"This only would I learn of you, Received ye the Spirit by the works of the law, or by the hearing of faith?"** And he says in verse 6. **"Even as Abraham believed God, and it was accounted to him for righteousness."**

And to nail the fact that mankind is saved by faith in Christ alone, he says the following in verse 11: **"But that no man is justified by the law in the sight of God, *it is* evident: for, The just shall live by faith."**

**Chapter 4, verses 13-15: "For the promise, that he should be the heir of the world, *was* not to Abraham, or to his seed, through the law, but through the righteousness of faith. For if they which are of the law *be* heirs, faith is made void, and the promise made of none effect: Because the law worketh wrath: for where no law is, *there is* no transgression."**

Abraham and Isaac and his subsequent seed were always going to be saved and justified by their faith in the one true God. Circumcision was a sign that they belonged to the Lord God of Israel, but circumcision in and of itself did not save them. Baptism does not save you; works do not save you.

And verse 15 makes it very clear how the law works wrath: **"for where no law is, *there is* no transgression."** The law shows you that you are a sinner; you are condemned by the law. And Paul said also in Galatians, chapter 3: **"Cursed *is* every one that continueth not in all things which are written in the book of the law to do them"** (Galatians 3:10). You are cursed if you don't keep the Old Testament law. And you are cursed if you try to keep it in order to be saved. Jesus Christ came to fulfil the law. Paul has to spend time after time dealing with this subject. The Jewish Judaizers were enemies of the cross. They hated the fact that mankind could be saved by believing in the Messiah. They wanted to add works to salvation. And Paul condemned those people; he wanted them cursed for adding works to the plan of salvation.

Do you know what the will of God is for your life? Please turn to Matthew, chapter 7. Look at verse 21, please: **"Not every one that saith unto me, Lord, Lord, shall enter into the** kingdom of heaven; but he that doeth the will of my Father which is in heaven. 22 Many will say to me in that day, Lord, Lord, have we not prophesied in thy name? and in thy name have cast out devils? and in thy name done many wonderful works?" Works, works, works!

Look at 23: **"And then will I profess unto them, I never knew you: depart from me, ye that work iniquity."** These people are commending themselves to the Lord based on their wonderful works, found in 22. They have died trusting in their wonderful works. And the Lord said: I never knew you; depart from me, ye workers of iniquity. These aren't going to be just some people at the Great White Throne. These are going to be many people at the Great White Throne. But He commends those that have done the will of His Father, found in verse 21.

So, what is the will of the Father? Please turn to John, chapter 6. Look at verse 40: **"And this is the will of him that sent me, that every one which seeth the Son, and believeth on him, may have everlasting life: and I will raise him up at the last day."** Look at 29: **"This is the work of God, that ye believe on him whom he hath sent."** The just shall live by faith. Pure and simple, one more time.

Please turn back to Romans, chapter 4. So, we are now halfway through chapter 4 of the Epistle to the Romans, and I showed you during the last broadcast how it was always the will of the Lord to save Jew and Gentile by faith alone. Pure and simple. The will of God was found clearly in John, chapter 6: to believe on the Lord Jesus Christ. It's not rocket science, it's very simple. And yet, this was a huge problem for the Jews because Paul was writing to the Gentiles in Rome while the temple was still in existence, and there were also saved Jews living in Rome who must also have been wondering what was going to happen to the Jews. The Messiah has been and gone, and for the most part Israel has not believed on Him. Hence, why Paul needed to write Romans and also why there was a need to write the Epistle to the Hebrews.

Has God finished with His people? Chapter 11 gives the answer.

But, for today, let's continue on, please, in verses 16:16-17: **"Therefore *it is* of faith, that *it might be* by grace; to the end the promise might be sure to all the seed; not to that only which is of the law, but to that also which is of the faith of Abraham; who is the father of us all, (As it is written, I have made thee a father of many nations,) before him whom he believed, *even* God, who quickeneth the dead, and calleth those things which be not as though they were."**

Abraham is the father of the Jew and also of the Gentile. Abraham got saved by faith alone; Isaac got saved by faith alone. There is no boasting here. When Abraham died and stood in the presence of the Lord Jesus Christ, he did not say I am here because I was a good man and I did A, B and C. When David died and entered into the presence of the Lord Jesus Christ, he didn't say I am here because I was a good man who did A, B and C. No! Abraham was saved without the deeds of the law. David was saved without the deeds of the law. You got saved without the deeds of the law. I got saved without the deeds of the law.

**VERSES 18-25:** "Who against hope believed in hope, that he might become the father of many nations, according to that which was spoken, So shall thy seed be. And being not weak in faith, he considered not his own body now dead, when he was about an hundred years old, neither yet the deadness of Sara's womb: He staggered not at the promise of God through unbelief; but was strong in faith, giving glory to God; And being fully persuaded that, what he had promised, he was able also to perform. And therefore it was imputed to him for righteousness. Now it was not written for his sake alone, that it was imputed to him; But for us also, to whom it shall be imputed, if we believe on him that raised up Jesus our Lord from the dead; Who was delivered for our offences, and was raised again for our justification."

So, verses 18 down to 25 prove conclusively how Abraham was saved by believing in the Lord. He was an old man, his wife was an old woman, and yet they both conceived Isaac as a result of the Lord's promise. It was a supernatural event, done deliberately to show man that he cannot save himself in and of himself.

And Paul says in verse 23, one more time: "**Now it was not written for his sake alone, that it was imputed to him; But for us also, to whom it shall be imputed, if we believe on him that raised up Jesus our Lord from the dead; Who was delivered for our offences, and was raised again for our justification.**" It can't be any clearer than this. If we believe on God who raised up Jesus from the dead, we are saved, we are justified, we are exonerated. No works involved. Paul has demonstrated and proved tirelessly and conclusively how Abraham was justified.

So, before I conclude this broadcast, I want to show you how the apostle Paul got saved. He's quoted Abraham, he's quoted David. But how did he get saved? Look at Acts, chapter 9, verse 5, please: **"And he said, Who art thou, Lord? And the Lord said, I am Jesus whom thou persecutest:** *it is* **hard for thee to kick against the pricks. 6 And he trembling and astonished said, Lord, what wilt thou have me to do? And the Lord** *said* **unto him, Arise, and go into the city, and it shall be told thee what thou must do."** Look at verse 17: **"And Ananias went his way, and entered into the house; and putting his hands on him said, Brother Saul, the Lord,** *even* **Jesus, that appeared unto thee in the way as thou camest, hath sent me, that thou mightest receive thy sight, and be filled with the Holy Ghost. 18 And immediately there fell from his eyes as it had been scales: and he received sight forthwith, and arose, and was baptized."**

Chapter 9, verse 6, Paul says to the Lord: what will you have me to do for you? I'm yours. He's been justified. In verse 17, Ananias is sent to Paul, and before he even baptizes Paul, he says, **"Brother Saul".** Paul has already been saved and justified. And by verse 18, he has been baptized. He got saved by faith in the Lord alone.

Genesis chapter 15, for Abraham. Acts chapter 9, for the apostle Paul. Acts 9, verse 4, Paul has been called to repent. Genesis chapter 12, verses 1, 2 and 3, Abraham has been called to repent. Acts 9, verse 18, Paul has now been baptized. Genesis chapter 17, Abraham was circumcised. The parallels, therefore, are clear to see. A man is justified by faith without the deeds of the law. **"Abraham believed God and it was counted unto him for righteousness... But to him that worketh not, but believeth on him that justifieth the ungodly, his faith is counted for righteousness"** (Romans 4:3,5). And one last and final time: faith alone, through grace alone, in Christ alone.

So, just before we get to chapter 5, I wanted to spend some time today looking at Romans chapter 4 where the apostle Paul makes it very clear how man is justified without the deeds of the law, whereas in James chapter 2, we are told that a sinner is saved by works and faith. And for many people, this causes great confusion. And it's quite understandable, but a little Bible study will hopefully, Lord willing, explain how Paul and James are both saying the same thing, but in different ways.

In Romans, chapter 4, verse 5, the apostle Paul says: **"But to him that worketh not, but believeth on him that justifieth the ungodly, his faith is counted for righteousness."** That's a very clear statement: **"to him that worketh not, but believeth on him that justifieth the ungodly, his faith is counted for righteousness."**

But look at James, chapter 2, verses 14-26: **"What *doth it* profit, my brethren, though a man say he hath faith, and have not works? can faith save him? If a brother or sister be naked, and destitute of daily food, And one of you say unto them, Depart in peace, be ye warmed and filled; notwithstanding ye give them not those things which are needful to the body; what *doth it* profit? Even so faith, if** it hath not works, is dead, being alone. Yea, a man may say, Thou hast faith, and I have works: shew me thy faith without thy works, and I will shew thee my faith by my works. Thou believest that there is one God; thou doest well: the devils also believe, and tremble. But wilt thou know, O vain man, that faith without works is dead? Was not Abraham our father justified by works, when he had offered Isaac his son upon the altar? Seest thou how faith wrought with his works, and by works was faith made perfect? And the scripture was fulfilled which saith, Abraham believed God, and it was imputed unto him for righteousness: and he was called the Friend of God. Ye see then how that by works a man is justified, and not by faith only. Likewise also was not Rahab the harlot justified by works, when she had received the messengers, and had sent *them* out another way? For as the body without the spirit is dead, so faith without works is dead also."

Verse 21 is the key to understanding the whole of James, chapter 2. When Abraham went to offer up Isaac his son, Isaac his son and the servants of Abraham saw what he was going to do. Abraham was saved before this event took place, but he was justified in the presence of Isaac and his servants. They saw his true faith, found in 15 and 16. A brother or sister is hungry and naked, and they want to have food, they need to be clothed. And a person who is saved demonstrates they are saved by doing good works. And Abraham is the definitive example of how a man gets saved and what he does once he is saved. He produces good works, of course.

Please turn to 1 Samuel chapter 16. Scripture with Scripture. Let's start in verses 6-7: **"And it came to pass, when they were come, that he looked on Eliab, and said, Surely the LORD'S anointed *is* before him. But the LORD said unto Samuel, Look not on his countenance, or on the height of his stature; because I have refused him: for *the LORD seeth* not as man seeth; for man looketh on the outward appearance, but the LORD looketh on the heart."** So, Romans 4 and James 2 are very easily reconcilable when you come to 1 Samuel chapter 16.

The Lord sees the heart of the penitent sinner, first of all, found in Romans chapter 4. And that man or that woman gets saved by believing on the Lord. Once a man is saved, he produces good works. Now his peers see his faith because his faith is demonstrated by good works, James chapter 2, of course. So, the Lord looks at the heart of man, Romans chapter 4, whereas man looks at the works of man, James chapter 2. Two Scriptures, both teaching the same thing, but in different ways. James is focusing on the works of a saved sinner, whereas Paul is focusing on a believer getting saved in the first place. Once you are saved, good works will follow. But you are not saved by your faith and your works. You are saved without the deeds of the law.

# CHAPTER 5

V ERSES 1-2: "Therefore being justified by faith, we have peace with God through our Lord Jesus Christ: By whom also we have access by faith into this grace wherein we stand, and rejoice in hope of the glory of God."

Chapter 5, verse 1 is a continuation from chapter 4, which I called: "The Faith Chapter". Abraham believed and it was accounted to him for righteousness. David believed and it was accounted unto him for righteousness. Chapter 5, verse 1, **"being justified by faith"** simply means you've been exonerated. You have been pardoned. You should go to Hell when you die because you have sinned, but the Lord made it possible to pardon all those sinners that believe on His Son. To have peace with God was unheard of in the Old Testament. If you wanted to be at peace with the Lord, you had to go to the temple, you had to offer up sacrifices. And the priest, most of the time, was your mediator. But now we go straight to the Father via the Lord Jesus Christ. Everything changed at Calvary, everything changed by the death, burial and resurrection of the Lord Jesus Christ. We have peace: P-E-A-C-E. Peace.

Bible Christianity is the only faith in the world that guarantees eternal life the moment a sinner believes on the Lord Jesus Christ. It is promised to you. It is guaranteed for you. It is in writing that you have been exonerated. No other faith, like I say, can guarantee this.

**VERSES 3-5: "And not only *so*, but we glory in tribulations also: knowing that tribulation worketh patience; And patience, experience; and experience, hope: And hope maketh not ashamed; because the love of God is shed abroad in our hearts by the Holy Ghost which is given unto us."**

Timothy was ashamed of the Lord, and eventually he got over that. In fact, he was martyred eventually for his faith in the Lord Jesus Christ. This term for being ashamed can also be in reference to your past sins. Most people that come to the Lord Jesus Christ have some history, meaning they lived in the world for "x" amount of years and they committed "x" amount of sins. That shame is always there, but by the death, burial and resurrection of the Lord Jesus Christ, it's all been done away with. You have been pardoned.

Tribulations also found in verse 3 are in reference to trials. If you are saved, you are going to go through trials and tribulations: a) to test your faith and b) to make you grow in grace so you can be an example and an encouragement to other people.

Please turn to Psalm 11, verse 5: **"The LORD trieth the righteous: but the wicked and him that loveth violence his soul hateth."** If you are a saved brother or sister in the Lord, and you are always going through trials and tribulations and you know of other people that claim to be saved but their life seems to be perfect, they seem to be pretty happy and content in what they are doing, then it's quite possible they are the wicked, they are the tares, they are the goats. Because if you are righteous, He is going to try you. In John 15, the Lord said He would prune those that were His.

Please turn back to Romans chapter 5. And also from verse 5, the term **"hope"** is not a blind hope. Our faith is substantiated in the Lord Jesus Christ and in the word of God. We have true faith, we have real hope in a person that lived 2,000 years ago, in a person that conquered death.

So, the overwhelming consensus from verse 3, 4 and 5 would be this: once you are saved, trials and tribulations are going to come, and by those trials and tribulations, a) the Lord can humble you and b) He can make you more aware of your brethren around the world. You can relate to their problems, and you can be a great comfort to them. But, ultimately from verse 5, you'll be content, you'll be equipped to do all things for Him. Why? Because the love of God is shed abroad in your hearts by the Holy Ghost. Amazing!

So, moving on through chapter 5, last time we saw how the man or woman of the Lord has now been justified freely by faith. And once they've been exonerated, once they've been pardoned, they now enjoy peace. Something which was unprecedented pre-4 B.C., when the Messiah was born, something that was unheard of pre-30 A.D., when the Lord hung on the cross. Mankind, pre the arrival of the Messiah, never quite knew if they were saved or not. They did their best to please the Lord, and they kept the law the best way they knew how. But they were never sure of salvation. But, now, in the New Covenant, we have access to the Father via the Lord Jesus Christ. It's guaranteed, it's promised, and we have it here in the word of God.

Look at verse 6, please:

**VERSE 6: "For when we were yet without strength, in due time Christ died for the ungodly."**

Please turn to Psalm, chapter 10. Look at verse 4: **"The wicked, through the pride of his countenance, will not seek *after God*: God *is* not in all his thoughts."** Man doesn't want the Lord. Man is at enmity with the Lord.

Please turn back to Romans chapter 5. Look at verse 6 one more time: **"For when we** [that's you and I] **were yet without strength** [meaning we were dead in our sins, we were the wicked found in Psalm chapter 10], **in due time** [30 A.D., He's hanging on the cross] **Christ died for the ungodly."** That's the whole world! Mankind, you and I!

**VERSE 7: "For scarcely for a righteous man will one die: yet peradventure for a good man some would even dare to die."**

That's very true, it's very rare for person A to die for person B. It has happened, but it's very rare. Yet Christ Jesus despised the shame, the King of the universe came down from Heaven and left His palace behind, and He was crucified for the sins of the world, found in Romans chapter 1, verse 18 down to 32. Every possible sin imaginable, He has atoned for. He was without sin, and by His death on the cross and our personal faith in Him, we can be saved.

Look at verse 8, please: **"But God commendeth his love toward us, in that, while we were yet sinners, Christ died for us."**

In verse 6, we are called ungodly and in verse 8, we are called sinners.

Please turn to Psalm chapter 14. Look at verse 1: **"The fool hath said in his heart, *There is* no God. They are corrupt, they have done abominable works, *there is* none that doeth good."** In chapter 10, verse 4, you are called wicked and chapter 14, verse 1, you are called a fool.

Please look back at Romans chapter 1. Look at verse 32: **"Who knowing the judgment of God, that they which commit such things are worthy of death, not only do the same, but have pleasure in them that do them."** These people are worthy of death. Please turn back to chapter 5, verse 8, one more time: **"But God commendeth his love toward us, in that, while we were yet sinners** [wicked, fools, worthy of death], **Christ died for us."** He is the bridge between God and man.

So, you have two options: you either accept Him and believe on Him and trust in Him as your Saviour or you reject Him and you face Him as your judge at the end of the world. The choice is yours. The Lord is a gentleman. He won't force Himself on you. But verse 8, one more time: **"But God commendeth his love toward us** [all of us], **in that, while we were yet sinners** [dead in our sins], **Christ died for us."** He loves you so much that He hung on a cross for six long, painful hours. But you have a free will. You either believe on Him or you do not. The ball is in your court.

So, let's start today's broadcast in verse 9: **"Much more then, being now justified by his blood, we shall be saved from wrath through him."**

Some teachers believe this is in reference to escaping the tribulation. It may be. But ultimately, I'm more of the opinion that this is in reference to escaping the judgment of God. Jesus has saved us from God ultimately.

In chapter 5, verse 1, the Scripture says **"being justified by faith"**. Faith in what? Found here in verse 9: faith in His blood, the precious blood of the Lamb.

Please turn to Acts chapter 20. Look at verse 28, please: **"Take heed therefore unto yourselves, and to all the flock, over the which the Holy Ghost hath made you overseers, to feed the Church of God, which he hath purchased with his own blood."** Jesus is God, found here very clearly. He purchased the Church with His own blood.

Please turn to 1 Peter. Some years ago I was talking to a rabbi about the Lord Jesus Christ and I took him to 1 Peter chapter 1, and I showed him verse 19 and the Scripture says, **"But with the precious blood of Christ, as of a lamb without blemish and without spot: Who verily was foreordained before the foundation of the world, but was manifest in these last times for you, Who by him do believe in God, that raised him up from the dead, and gave him glory; that your faith**

**and hope might be in God"** and I said to this rabbi, we are saved by the precious blood of the Lord Jesus Christ. And he just looked at me. But it's a fact. We were saved by the precious blood of the Lord Jesus Christ, found here very clearly in 1 Peter and found in Acts chapter 20 to be God's blood.

Please turn back to Romans chapter 5: to be justified, which means to be exonerated, which means to be pardoned, by His blood, found in verse 9, through Him proves once and for all that salvation is a free gift. You weren't justified by being baptized. You were justified by His blood. And you are going to be saved through Him. He is a living Saviour; He is alive today. He may have died on the cross, but the triune God resurrected Him. And He is alive today. So, verse 9 should be underlined in all of your Bibles. One more time: **"being now justified by his blood, we shall be saved from wrath through him."** We board the Lord Jesus Christ. He is our ark. He is the captain of our salvation. We are safe in Him. He is our refuge, He is our high tower. But you have to believe on Him. **"The just shall live by faith."**

**Chapter 5, verse 10: "For if, when we were enemies, we were reconciled to God by the death of his Son, much more, being reconciled, we shall be saved by his life."**

Please turn back to Romans chapter 1. Look at verse 20: **"For the invisible things of him from the creation of the world are clearly seen, being understood by the things that are made, *even* his eternal power and Godhead; so that they are without excuse: Because that, when they knew God, they glorified *him* not as God, neither were thankful; but** became vain in their imaginations, and their foolish heart was darkened. Professing themselves to be wise, they became fools, And changed the glory of the uncorruptible God into an image made like to corruptible man, and to birds, and fourfooted beasts, and creeping things." It's like evolution here. They know him from the creation of the world, found in verse 20. They are without excuse, from verse 21. In verse 22, they profess to be wise but they are fools. Psalm 14: "The fool hath said in his heart, *There is* no God." found here in Romans chapter 1. And by verse 23, they have changed the glory of the uncorruptible, the beautiful, the holy, the righteous God into an image made like to corruptible man and to birds and four-footed beasts and creeping things.

Evolution! They defile God's glory. They deny that God is God, they deny that God made everything.

Please turn back to chapter 5, verse 10, one more time: **"For if, when we** [that's you and I] **were enemies, we were reconciled to God by the death of his Son** [He's made it possible to save all of us, 2 Corinthians, chapter 5, verse 19]: **"God was in Christ, reconciling the world unto himself, not imputing their trespasses unto them; and hath committed unto us the word of reconciliation"**, **"much more, being reconciled, we shall be saved by his life."**

God has made a provision to save everyone. But you have to appropriate the atonement. "The just shall live by faith". You have to call on the name of the Lord. God be merciful to me, a sinner. And He will save you in a flash. He died for the ungodly in verse 6, He died for sinners in verse 8, and He died for His enemies in verse 10. What more does He need to do?

Please turn to Psalm chapter 7 and look at verse 11: **"God judgeth the righteous, and God is angry *with the wicked every day.*"** We found tribulations and trials in Romans chapter 5, verse 3, and here, not only does he judge the righteous, the saved people, but He is angry with the wicked every day.

Look at Psalm chapter 5, verse 5: **"The foolish shall not stand in thy sight: thou hatest all workers of iniquity."** You won't stand in His sight. You'll be on your face when He judges you as the Judge of the universe. He hates all workers of iniquity. Look at Psalm 9, verse 17: **"The wicked shall be turned into hell, and all the nations that forget God."**

Please turn back to Romans, chapter 5. Very quickly. He's either going to be your Saviour or your Judge. He has died for those people found in Psalm 7, 9, 10 and 14. But now He waits patiently as a Saviour. He is longsuffering, He is not willing that any should perish but that all should come to repentance.

Let's conclude this broadcast, if we may, in verse 11. **"And not only *so*, but we also joy in God through our Lord Jesus Christ, by whom we have now received the atonement."**

Present tense. We have now received the atonement. **"Father, into thy hands I commend my spirit"** (Luke 23:46). It is done, it is finished, it has been accomplished! **"Behold, now *is* the accepted time; behold, now *is* the day of salvation"** (2 Corinthians chapter 6, verse 2). **"Be ye reconciled unto Him"** (2 Corinthians 5:20). And that is God's plan for man. **"The**

**Son of Man is come to seek and save that which was lost"** (Luke 19:10).

Okay, so before I get to verse 12, I wanted to spend some time today looking at the atonement. I've shown you from previous broadcasts how man is universally depraved and how man will not seek the Lord, not that he cannot seek the Lord, but that he chooses not to seek the Lord. At the same time, the Lord is holy, the Lord is righteous, the Lord is a perfectionist. He cannot lower His standard. Therefore, we have a dilemma. How can God be reconciled to man? And what exactly is the atonement? For the Lord to lower His standard would mean the Lord is no longer the Lord. For unsaved people to enter into Heaven upon death would mean something seriously wrong has occurred. What exactly, therefore, is the atonement?

Please turn to Luke chapter 7. Let's start in verse 36: **"And one of the Pharisees desired him that he would eat with him. And he went into the Pharisee's house, and sat down to meat. And, behold, a woman in the city, which was a sinner, when she knew that Jesus sat at meat in the Pharisee's house, brought an alabaster box of ointment, And stood at his feet behind _him_ weeping, and began to wash his feet with tears, and did wipe _them_ with the hairs of her head, and kissed his feet, and anointed _them_ with the ointment."** This woman found in verse 37 is a sinner, but more precisely, she's a prostitute. And she plucks up the courage to enter the house of the Pharisee with all of his cohorts. Can you imagine how hard that must have been for her? Before she walks into the room, she is already saved.

Romans chapter 4, the Lord sees the heart of the penitent sinner, first and foremost; then He justifies that sinner. And James chapter 2, man sees the works of a saved sinner.

I showed you from 1 Samuel chapter 16 how the Lord looks on the heart, Romans chapter 4, whereas man looks on the outward appearance (James chapter 2). Luke chapter 7, verse 39: **"Now when the Pharisee which had bidden him saw *it*, he spake within himself, saying, This man, if he were a prophet, would have known who and what manner of woman *this is* that toucheth him: for she is a sinner."** Two points from verse 39: the Pharisee says if the Lord was a prophet, He wouldn't allow this woman who was a sinner, meaning she was an immoral woman, to touch Him. To touch a priest or to touch a prophet in the Old Testament was out. If you were unclean, you couldn't even look at the high priest and yet here, this woman, an immoral woman, has been able to touch the Lord. And this self-righteous Pharisee is incredulous.

Look at verse 40: **"And Jesus answering said unto him, Simon, I have somewhat to say unto thee."** So, this verse demonstrates the omniscience of the Lord Jesus Christ. Deity! **"And he saith, Master, say on. There was a certain creditor which had two debtors: the one owed five hundred pence, and the other fifty. And when they had nothing to pay, he frankly forgave them both. Tell me therefore, which of them will love him most?"** The wisdom here of the Lord Jesus Christ surpasses the wisdom of Solomon, and Simon must be aware that the Lord Jesus is referring to him and the woman.

Verse 43: "**Simon answered and said, I suppose that *he*, to whom he forgave most. And he said unto him, Thou hast rightly judged. And he turned to the woman, and said unto Simon, Seest thou this woman? I entered into thine house, thou gavest me no water for my feet: but she hath washed my feet with tears, and wiped *them* with the hairs of her head. Thou gavest me no kiss: but this woman since the time I came in hath not ceased to kiss my feet. My head with oil thou didst not anoint: but this woman hath anointed my feet with ointment. Wherefore I say unto thee, Her sins, which are many, are forgiven; for she loved much: but to whom little is forgiven, *the same* loveth little.**" Her sins were great, her sins were many, as were his sins! He was a Pharisee, he was an upright member of the community. And the Lord says one more time: "**but to whom little is forgiven, *the same* loveth little.**" Simon was a self-righteous Pharisee, whereas this woman, on the other hand, was a humble sinner. These two couldn't have been further apart.

Look at verse 48: "**And he said unto her, Thy sins are forgiven.**" He's the Lord of the temple, He's the Lord of the Sabbath, He's deity. Only God can forgive sins. Your sins are forgiven. "The just shall live by faith". No works needed.

Verse 49: "**And they that sat at meat with him began to say within themselves, Who is this that forgiveth sins also?**" Who is this man that can raise the dead, who is this man that can still the waves, calm the storm, give sight to the blind. They didn't have a clue as to who He was. Who is this Man that forgiveth sins also? And by this stage He doesn't even respond to their questions. He knew what they were thinking, He is omniscient, He is omnipresent, and He's omnipotent.

But His focus here is on the lady. A saved sinner. And He concludes this in verse 50: **"And he said to the woman, Thy faith hath saved thee; go in peace."** P-E-A-C-E. Peace. Found in Romans chapter 5, verse 1.

So, that in a nutshell, is what the atonement is. She believed on the Lord (Romans chapter 4), she went into the Pharisee's house and she demonstrated her faith in the Lord, which was seen among the Pharisees and also from the Lord Jesus Christ (James chapter 2). She was justified by her works in the presence of those present on that occasion. Abraham was saved (Romans chapter 4) and when he went to offer up Isaac his son, he was justified by his works in the presence of Isaac his son. So, Romans 4 and James chapter 2 are completely in harmony with one another, but they are focusing on the atonement from two different perspectives. **"The just shall live by faith".**

So, during the last broadcast, we looked at the atonement and we discovered just how magnificent, just how marvellous, just how loving the Lord God of the Bible really is. In your worst possible state, He died for your very sins. He knew before you were even born what sins you would have committed before you got saved and even after you got saved. And yet He still died for you nevertheless. So, just rest in the Lord Jesus Christ and if you have sin in your life, just confess it to Him, and He – Christ Jesus – is faithful and just to forgive you of all of your sins. So, just rest in Him!

So, let's start today's broadcast, if we may, in verses 12-13: **"Wherefore, as by one man sin entered into the world, and death by sin; and so death passed upon all men, for that all have sinned: (For until the law sin was in the world: but sin is not imputed when there is no law."**

Two points from verse 12: Adam's sin caused him to die spiritually. All men, Jew and Gentile, are therefore dead in their sins until they are born again. So, with all men being in their sins, all men need a Saviour. Period. And original sin, for those that don't know, is the knowledge of good and evil. Mankind in general is a sinner. We all fall short of the glory of God. There is not a just man upon the face of the earth. Nobody is good but God. And two points from verse 13: Sin was in the world even before the law came. So, nobody is going to escape God's judgment on sin. And also sin is not imputed when there is no law. We that are saved today are not under the law. We have been saved from the law. We have been saved from our sins. We have been saved from Hell. We have been saved from God's wrath. We are not under the law. Therefore, sin cannot touch us. Sin and the law are not going to be imputed unto us. Why? Because Christ has died for our sins. He is the perfect Lamb of God.

So, moving on through chapter 5 of the Epistle to the Romans, and last time we saw how sin is a universal problem. Jew and Gentile are all under the curse of the law. They are all born in original sin. They are all going to face God's judgment, if they are not born again.

Let's start today's broadcast in verse 14: **"Nevertheless death reigned from Adam to Moses, even over them that had not sinned after the similitude of Adam's transgression, who is the figure of him that was to come."**

Adam was created perfect and upright. He wasn't sinless, but due to his fall, mankind now knows the difference between right and wrong, which is what original sin is. So, although Adam's sons and daughters weren't guilty, *per se*, of his original sin with Eve, they have suffered the consequences of their parents' sin. And we have all suffered the consequences of Adam and Eve's sin. But the verse ends on a good note when it says he was the figure of Him that was to come, meaning the Lord Jesus Christ. Adam fell and everything went into decay, but Christ came and restored humanity. Adam lost paradise; Jesus has regained paradise.

**Chapter 5, verse 15: "But not as the offence, so also *is* the free gift. For if through the offence of one many be dead, much more the grace of God, and the gift by grace, *which is* by one man, Jesus Christ, hath abounded unto many."**

**"Free gift"** in verse 15 should be underlined. Salvation, one more time, is a free gift. Paul says in verse 15 that many be dead. All and many are used interchangeably. They mean the same thing. Verse 12: Death passed upon all men. Verse 14: Death reigned from Adam to Moses. Verse 15: Many, meaning all, are dead in their sins. And Jesus' death, burial and resurrection has abounded unto many. Again, many meaning all. And the latter verses prove this.

**VERSE 16: "And not as *it was* by one that sinned, so is the gift: for the judgment was by one to condemnation, but the free gift *is* of many offences unto justification."**

That word again for justification means exoneration. It means to be pardoned. Judgment equals condemnation, which equals everlasting Hell. Who is it for? All men. Why? Because death has passed upon all men, found very clearly in verse 12. But verse 16 ends on a good note: **"but the free gift"**, meaning you can't work for it, meaning you cannot earn it, meaning you cannot lose it either. **"But the free gift *is* of many offences unto justification."** Adam's sin and his treason caused him to die spiritually, and the avalanche of sin which has come since that day was nailed ultimately to the cross of the Lord Jesus Christ. He despised the shame, and He conquered sin and death for all of us.

We are nearly halfway through chapter 5, and this is where Paul, the theologian, shines. Paul was a genius when it came to explaining the atonement: a man's problem being sin, but the remedy being Jesus Christ.

Let's start today's broadcast in verses 17-21: **"For if by one man's offence death reigned by one; much more they which receive abundance of grace and of the gift of righteousness shall reign in life by one, Jesus Christ.) Therefore as by the offence of one *judgment came* upon all men to condemnation; even so by the righteousness of one *the free gift came* upon all men unto justification of life. For as by one man's disobedience many were made sinners, so by the obedience of one shall many be made righteous. Moreover** the law entered, that the offence might abound. But where sin abounded, grace did much more abound: That as sin hath reigned unto death, even so might grace reign through righteousness unto eternal life by Jesus Christ our Lord."

In verse 17, Adam's sin resulted in the death of the human race. But to those that **"receive the abundance of grace and of the gift of righteousness"** through the Lord Jesus Christ shall reign with Him. Here and now!

Verse 18: Judgment came upon everyone. Verse 19, through Adam's disobedience came Christ's obedience. Where Adam fell through his disobedience, Christ was victorious through His obedience. In verse 20, the law points to judgment, **but "where sin abounded, grace did much more abound"**. In verse 21, sin reigns unto death. Sin will take you to Hell forever, but Jesus Christ has abolished death. He has conquered sin. And for you to receive eternal life, you need to believe on Him, and then He becomes your Lord.

# CHAPTER 6

---

VERSE 1: "What shall we say then? Shall we continue in sin, that grace may abound?"

Paul knows he's going to get some flak for teaching very clearly and firmly how we are no longer under the law. We've been saved from the law, we have been saved from sin.

In chapter 3, verse 8, Paul said the following: **"And not *rather*, (as we be slanderously reported, and as some affirm that we say,) Let us do evil, that good may come? whose damnation is just."** Like I say, for those of us that hold to eternal security, we too are slanderously reported to somehow be teaching people to sin as they will, because all of your past, present and future sins have been forgiven. But that's not true! We don't teach people to go out and live as they choose. And Paul had the same issue to deal with.

**Chapter 6, verse 2: "God forbid. How shall we, that are dead to sin, live any longer therein?"**

Not sinless! We haven't yet reached perfection, but we are dead to sin, we are dead to the law. Why? Because Jesus Christ has paid for our very sins.

Chapter 5, verse 13: **"but sin is not imputed when there is no law." "God was in Christ reconciling the world unto Himself, not imputing their sins unto them"** (2 Cor. 5:19).

So, just to prove that we are not yet sinless, please turn to 1 John chapter 1. Look at verse 8: **"If we say that we have no sin, we deceive ourselves, and the truth is not in us."** Look at verse 10: **"If we say that we have not sinned, we make him a liar, and his word is not in us."**

Please turn to Philippians chapter 3 one more time. Look at verse 12, Paul speaking: **"Not as though I had already attained, either were already perfect: but I follow after, if that I may apprehend that for which also I am apprehended of Christ Jesus."** Perfect here means complete, it means sinless. He was still living in his cursed body in a cursed world. He wasn't sinless. You are not sinless, and I am not sinless. Not yet, anyway! When we die, yes, but for here and now, no.

Please turn back to Romans chapter 6. So, during the last broadcast, we found very clearly how we are dead to sin. We are dead to the law. Why? Because Christ has paid for our very sins on the cross. We are not sinless, but we are dead to sin. The law, therefore, cannot touch us. Sin, therefore, cannot touch us. And Paul knows he's going to be attacked for teaching this. He knew that the Judaizers were going to come against him, as were other ignorant people, but he pushed on, nevertheless.

Look at verse 3: **"Know ye not, that so many of us as were baptized into Jesus Christ were baptized into his death?"**

**"Many of us"**, meaning for those that have appropriated the atonement. **"Many"** meaning all, all without exception. All of us that are born again have been baptized into Jesus Christ. Not a water baptism, but a spiritual baptism.

Please turn to 1 Corinthians, chapter 12. Look at verse 13: **"For by one Spirit are we all baptized into one body, whether *we be* Jews or Gentiles, whether *we be* bond or free; and have been all made to drink into one Spirit."** Water wasn't mentioned once.

Please turn to Ephesians chapter 4, verse 4: **"*There is* one body, and one Spirit, even as ye are called in one hope of your calling; One Lord, one faith, one baptism, One God and Father of all, who *is* above all, and through all, and in you all."** One Lord, one faith, one baptism! When you got saved, you were baptized by the Holy Spirit into Jesus Christ. A spiritual baptism, not a water baptism.

Please turn back to Romans chapter 6. So, should you be baptized once you are born again? Absolutely, if possible by total immersion. But water does not save you. Water puts you into water. The Spirit puts you into the Spirit. The Spirit puts you into Jesus Christ. His body. Get baptized once you are saved, but baptism in and of itself does not save you.

Look at verse 4: **"Therefore we are buried with him by baptism into death: that like as Christ was raised up from the dead by the glory of the Father, even so we also should walk in newness of life."**

Were you buried with the Lord Jesus Christ literally? The answer, of course, is no. But, spiritually speaking you were. When He hung on the cross, all of your sins were put to His account. And by His precious blood, you are now forgiven. So, spiritually speaking, yes, you were buried with Him. Yes, you were baptized into Him. Not physically, not literally, but spiritually speaking. Letterism is something which, unfortunately, many Christians fall into. They take every verse of the Bible to be literal, which is very dangerous. Verse 4 is speaking about your new birth. You went down with Him and you came up with Him. And now you walk in the newness of life. It's in reference to the new birth, that's all.

**VERSE 5-7: "For if we have been planted together in the likeness of his death, we shall be also *in the likeness* of *his* resurrection: Knowing this, that our old man is crucified with *him*, that the body of sin might be destroyed, that henceforth we should not serve sin. For he that is dead is freed from sin."**

Verse 5: We are going to look like the Lord Jesus Christ when He comes back. We are going to have glorified bodies.

But verses 6 and 7 are in reference to putting yourself back under the law, like the Galatians did. They were trying to somehow revive their old natures, their old bodies. They were trying to go back to how they used to be by putting themselves back under the law. They were never under the law to begin with! They weren't even Jews! But by going back to the law, they were serving sin. And yet, they are dead to sin, they are dead to the law. "*There is* **therefore now no condemnation to them which are in Christ Jesus**" (Romans 8:1). Verse 6: **"Knowing this** [don't you know, I've already told you] **that our old man is crucified with *him*"**. Not literally, one more time. You weren't literally nailed to the cross with Him. Spiritually speaking, you were. Symbolically speaking, you were, but not physically, not literally. Again, letterism! Be careful not to fall into that trap.

And he goes on to say, **"that the body of sin might be destroyed, that henceforth we** [all of us] **should not serve sin."** He abolished death and He has fulfilled the law. The woman caught in the act of adultery was told to go and sin no more! She got saved by believing on Him. Faith alone! The just shall live by faith! She wasn't baptized and she wasn't a member of any church either. She believed on Him and it was counted unto her for righteousness.

Verse 7 one more time: **"For he that is dead is freed from sin."** You died with Him; you were baptized into Him, and you were resurrected with Him. Go and sin no more! **"The just shall live by faith!"** It's so simply and yet sadly, it's lost on so many people.

**VERSES 8-9: "Now if we be dead with Christ, we believe that we shall also live with him: Knowing that Christ being raised from the dead dieth no more; death hath no more dominion over him."**

To be dead with him, from verse 8, means to be identified with Him, not physically dead, but spiritually dead. And once we are made alive through the new birth, we live with Him, we live in Him. He is our being. We can do nothing without Him. Verse 9: **"Knowing that Christ being raised from the dead dieth no more".** The Lamb of God was sacrificed for the sins of the world just once. Pre the arrival of the Lord Jesus Christ, animals were being sacrificed all of the time for the sins of those that came to have their sins atoned for. The priests were always standing because their work was never done. It was an ongoing sacrifice. But Jesus has sat down at the right hand of the Father. It is finished. It is done.

Look at verse 10: **"For in that he died, he died unto sin once: but in that he liveth, he liveth unto God."**

Died once, past tense. Liveth in the present tense. The Roman Catholic Church teaches that the mass is an ongoing commission; it is an ongoing sacrifice. But that's not what we found in Romans chapter 6.

Please turn to Hebrews chapter 7. Look at verse 25: **"Wherefore he is able also to save them to the uttermost that come unto God by him, seeing he ever liveth to make intercession for them."** Once saved, always saved. He will save you to the uttermost without any works.

Look at verse 26: **"For such an high priest became us, *who is* holy, harmless, undefiled, separate from sinners, and made higher than the heavens; Who needeth not daily, as those high priests, to offer up sacrifice, first for his own sins, and then for the people's: for this he did once, when he offered up himself."** A one and only sacrifice. Period. The priests offered up sacrifices for themselves. But not Him! He was without sin.

Look at chapter 9, verse 22: **"And almost all things are by the law purged with blood; and without shedding of blood is no remission."** His physical, literal blood atoned for our sins. Period!

Look at verse 28: **"So Christ was once offered to bear the sins of many; and unto them that look for him shall he appear the second time without sin unto salvation."** It was a one-off atonement.

Look at verse 12: **"Neither by the blood of goats and calves, but by his own blood he entered in once into the holy place, having obtained eternal redemption *for us*."** Salvation is eternal. And He went into the Holy of Holies just once! That's all it needed.

Look at chapter 10, verse 14: **"For by one offering he hath perfected for ever them that are sanctified."** It can't be any clearer. He died for the sins of the world once, and only once.

So, please turn back to Romans chapter 6, verse 10, one more time: **"For in that he died, he died unto sin once: but in that he liveth, he liveth unto God."** The mass is not needed, the mass is irrelevant. We are saved by His death, burial and resurrection. Without the shedding of blood, there is no remission of sins. We are saved, therefore, by the precious blood of the Lamb of God.

Also from verse 10: **"in that he liveth, he liveth unto God."** His work as our Mediator is an ongoing work. He mediates on our behalf. When we pray to Him, He intercedes for us. So, His work as our High Priest is an ongoing work. It's an ongoing commission.

But, His atonement was a one-off event. So, verse 10, one more time: **"in that he liveth** [present tense]**, he liveth** [present tense] **unto God."** He is our Mediator between God and Man.

**Chapter 6, verse 11: "Likewise reckon ye also yourselves to be dead indeed unto sin, but alive unto God through Jesus Christ our Lord."**

You can take verse 11 and apply it to those of us living today in reference to not feeding the old man, not living according to the flesh, not being carnal. Absolutely! But, primarily, Paul is speaking about your practical standing as far as the Lord is concerned. Don't go back to the law. Stop feeding the old nature. Stop trying to resurrect the dead man. Christ died once for your sins and now you are identified with Him. You were buried with Him once, you were baptized with Him once and you were resurrected with Him once. You were born again once. So, leave the old man in the ground and now walk in the newness of life.

**Chapter 6, verse 12: "Let not sin therefore reign in your mortal body, that ye should obey it in the lusts thereof."**

You are in charge of your body. So, don't feed the flesh. Don't let sin reign in your mortal body, because if you feed the flesh, you will die. You will die physically and you will may even die prematurely. So, walk in the Spirit and not in the flesh.

**VERSE 13: "Neither yield ye your members *as* instruments of unrighteousness unto sin: but yield yourselves unto God, as those that are alive from the dead, and your members as instruments of righteousness unto God."**

Be a slave to holiness, be a slave to righteousness. Be a rebel against sin. Live unto Him, not to yourself. Why? Because you are saved and the Lord God is your Master.

In chapter 2, verse 24, Paul said the following: **"For the name of God is blasphemed among the Gentiles through you, as it is written."** Ungodly, unholy and self-righteous Jews were causing the Gentiles to blaspheme God.

So, back in chapter 6, verse 13, Paul says: No, don't you do that! You are no longer a slave to sin, you are a slave to righteousness. You were purchased with a price. You belong to your Master, the Lord Jesus Christ. He owns you! So, don't make provisions for the flesh or for sin. Be a rebel against sin, but be righteous unto Him.

**VERSE 14: "For sin shall not have dominion over you: for ye are not under the law, but under grace."**

Don't become legalistic like the Galatians did. Don't become carnal like the Corinthians did. The old man, the old nature, died with Christ. So, be ye holy unto the Lord. Live for Him, not for yourself.

**VERSES 15-23: "What then? shall we sin, because we are not under the law, but under grace? God forbid. Know ye not, that to whom ye yield yourselves servants to obey, his servants ye are to whom ye obey; whether of sin unto death, or of obedience unto righteousness? But God be thanked, that ye were the servants of sin, but ye have obeyed from the heart that form of doctrine which was delivered you. Being then made free from sin, ye became the servants of righteousness. I speak after the manner of men because of the infirmity of your flesh: for as ye have yielded your members servants to uncleanness and to iniquity unto**

iniquity; even so now yield your members servants to righteousness unto holiness. For when ye were the servants of sin, ye were free from righteousness. What fruit had ye then in those things whereof ye are now ashamed? for the end of those things is death. But now being made free from sin, and become servants to God, ye have your fruit unto holiness, and the end everlasting life. For the wages of sin *is* death; but the gift of God *is* eternal life through Jesus Christ our Lord."

In verse 15, Paul condemns those that would live after the flesh because they are now living under the covenant of grace. And he says, God forbid! May it never be! In verse 16, he says, don't you know that to whom you serve, to them you become their servants. Whether of sin unto death or obedience unto righteousness. You cannot serve two masters.

Verse 17: **God be thanked! "that ye were** [past tense] **the servants of sin, but ye** [all of you] **have obeyed** [by faith alone] **from the heart that form of doctrine which was delivered you."** Bible-believing Christians! We believed in our heart that Jesus is God, that He died for our sins and we believe in the word of God. God be thanked! Praise His name! Glorify Him!

Verses 18, 19 and 20 continue to build on the main theme of chapter 6. You're not under the law, you are under grace. So push on, move on!

In verse 21, he asks: What fruit did you have that caused you to become ashamed? (Chapter 1, verses 18 down to 32). Please read it again: **"for the end of those things *is* death!"**

Verse 22: But now that you are born again, **"being made free from sin** [past tense] **and become servants [not slaves] to God** [present tense]**, ye have your fruit unto holiness, and the end everlasting life."** What a gracious Saviour! What a merciful God!

**"For the wages** [payment] **of sin *is* death"** (verse 23): physical death and also spiritual death. You reap what you sow! **"But the gift of God *is* eternal life through Jesus Christ our Lord." "I am the way, the truth, and the life: no man cometh unto the Father, but by me"** (John 14:6). And those four words, **"our Lord, our Saviour"** are only applicable if you have believed on Him. **"The just shall live by faith!"**

# CHAPTER 7

VERSES 1-3: "Know ye not, brethren, (for I speak to them that know the law,) how that the law hath dominion over a man as long as he liveth? For the woman which hath an husband is bound by the law to *her* husband so long as he liveth; but if the husband be dead, she is loosed from the law of *her* husband. So then if, while *her* husband liveth, she be married to another man, she shall be called an adulteress: but if her husband be dead, she is free from that law; so that she is no adulteress, though she be married to another man."

Chapter 7, verse 1: "**Know ye not, brethren** [don't you all know, brothers?] **(for I speak to them that know the law,)**" in reference to the Jews, of course. Here, Paul is acting like a prosecuting attorney. In chapter 5 and chapter 6, he made it very clear that the law cannot save you. And here, he's going to use a very clever analogy. In verse 1, he says that the law has dominion over a man as long as he lives, from the cradle to the grave! Dominion, submission, authority. He's going to prove conclusively to the Judaizers that as long as a person lives, if they are not saved, they are under the law.

But chapter 6, verse 23, told us, **"For the wages of sin *is* death"**. Chapter 6, verse 2, **"How shall we, that are dead to sin, live any longer therein?"**

Chapter 5, verse 13, **"But sin is not imputed when there is no law."** Chapter 6, verse 3, **"Know ye not, that so many of us as were baptized into Jesus Christ were baptized into his death?"** Baptized, buried and resurrected with Him. So, for the Church, the law is dead, it is obsolete.

Chapter 7, verses 2 and 3, he makes it very clear that, for a married couple, living under the law, that marriage could only be annulled at death. And if the wife left her husband and married another man, she would be called an adulteress, which meant death in the Old Testament. So, what is Paul telling us? A man meets a woman and gets married. And according to the law, she cannot divorce him. She cannot leave him until he is dead. According to the Old Testament. Chapter 7, verse 1: **"I speak to them that know the law".** Old Testament teachings. 'Til death do us part. But for the New Covenant, the Church marries the Lord Jesus Christ. 'Til death do us part. So, for a saved party to go back to the law would mean that he/she has committed adultery. They have fallen from grace.

**VERSE 4: "Wherefore, my brethren, ye also are become dead to the law by the body of Christ; that ye should be married to another, *even* to him who is raised from the dead, that we should bring forth fruit unto God."**

This chapter, ultimately, is the grand finale. Paul, like I said, is acting like a prosecuting attorney and he is saying that the law has found you guilty before Almighty God and the consequences, one more time, from chapter 6, verse 23: **"For the wages [payment for your sins against God] of sin *is* death [physical death]; but the gift of God *is* eternal life**

**through Jesus Christ our Lord."** Now, he's acting as a defence attorney. Paul was a mastermind when it came to the things of God.

But, look at chapter 7, verse 4, one more time: **"Wherefore, my brethren** [my brothers], **ye also are become dead to the law."** How? **"By the body of Christ; that ye** [all of you] **should be married to another, *even* to him who is raised from the dead, that we** [all of us] **should bring forth fruit unto God."**

Walk in the Spirit, not in the flesh. The fruits of the Spirit are a sign that you are growing in grace, and he is still referring to this brilliant analogy of how the Church has been married to Christ. The Church is under grace, not the law. Jesus Christ died for our sins. He has abolished the law, He has fulfilled the law. Therefore, we live unto Him, not unto ourselves.

**VERSES 5-6: "For when we were in the flesh, the motions of sins, which were by the law, did work in our members to bring forth fruit unto death. But now we are delivered from the law, that being dead wherein we were held; that we should serve in newness of spirit, and not *in* the oldness of the letter."**

Verses 5 and 6 are very clear: once again, in reference to chapter 6, verse 23. Before we got saved, we were dead in our sins. We were enemies of God. We didn't seek after Him. But, thankfully, He sought after us and found us and saved us. And also from 5 and 6 he was referring to the Jews that were trying to keep the law and yet they were killing themselves because the law kills, but the Spirit makes you alive.

**VERSE 7: "What shall we say then? *Is* the law sin? God forbid. Nay, I had not known sin, but by the law: for I had not known lust, except the law had said, Thou shalt not covet."**

Paul is pre-empting the response that he knows he's going to come from the Jews. The Jews are going to say to Paul, Are you saying that the law is sinful? And he says, No! God forbid! I wouldn't have known it was sinful to lust if it hadn't have been found in the Scriptures. Paul loved the Lord and Paul loved the law. But he knew that the law couldn't save you, it kills you! Only the Spirit, via the new birth, can make you alive. Also, he's not telling us that he didn't know the difference between right and wrong if it hadn't been for the Scriptures, because he had a conscience. And Romans chapter 1, verse 18 down to 32, make it very clear that mankind universally knows the difference between right and wrong. He's upholding the law; he's elevating the law. But, at the same time, he's still wearing his prosecuting attorney's hat.

**VERSES 8-9: "But sin, taking occasion by the commandment, wrought in me all manner of concupiscence. For without the law sin was dead. For I was alive without the law once: but when the commandment came, sin revived, and I died."**

Not physically, of course, but spiritually, of course!

**Chapter 7, verse 10: "And the commandment, which *was ordained* to life, I found *to be* unto death."**

It can't be any clearer! The law kills you. The law convicts you. The law destroys you. The law is a schoolmaster to bring us to Christ. Paul was a righteous man; Paul was a godly man. And Paul was an educated man. But he says one more time, from verse 9: **"sin revived, and I died."**

Had it been possible for Paul to have kept the law, he would have kept it. But Abraham couldn't keep it, and David couldn't keep it. Only one Person kept the law perfect. The second Adam. The Lord Jesus Christ! Why? Because He is God Almighty.

**VERSES 11-12: "For sin, taking occasion by the commandment, deceived me, and by it slew me. Wherefore the law *is* holy, and the commandment holy, and just, and good."**

Why? Because it came from God. God is holy. He cannot lower His standards. He cannot compromise on sin. Therefore, man has a problem. God is holy, man is not. What is the solution? The Lord Jesus Christ, of course! Also from verse 9, Paul says that he was alive without the law once, but when the commandment came, sin revived and he died, meaning he came to the age of accountability. And at that stage, he was convicted. He was under the law. And as a result, and as a consequence, of coming of age, of now being accountable to the Lord, he said in verse 11 that the law slew him. Again, not physically, but spiritually speaking. And just before I sign off from this broadcast, one quick footnote, if I may. Chapter 5, verse 13, one more time: **"For until the law sin was in the world: but sin is not imputed when there is no law",** meaning until you come of age, the law won't touch you. Sin won't condemn you. If you die before the age of accountability, you won't go to Hell, you will go to Heaven. Why? Because you're not yet old enough to know the difference between right and wrong. And therefore, Jesus Christ has substitutionally saved you from your sin. I am referring, of course, to infants and mentally impaired people. Called the innocents in the Old Testament. **"Suffer the little children to come unto me, and forbid them not: for of such is the kingdom of heaven"** (Mark 10:14).

**VERSE 13: "Was then that which is good made death unto me? God forbid. But sin, that it might appear sin, working death in me by that which is good; that sin by the commandment might become exceeding sinful."**

I died (verse 9), it slew me (verse 11) and by 13, it became exceeding sinful. What is he speaking about? a) the law and b) his flesh. He was born in sin. I was born in sin. You are born in sin. We are all born in sin. We have all fallen short of the glory of God and we all continue to fall short of the glory of God. Paul in his role as a prosecuting attorney has just put himself on the stand. If you've sinned against God, only God Himself can forgive you. The law cannot save you. There is no atonement within the law. And when a saved person tries to keep the law, he/she falls from grace. They dishonour the Lord. So, if the law cannot save you, what can? The death, burial and resurrection of the Lord Jesus Christ. And from verses 14 down to 25, Paul is going to become a defence attorney, because he too needed an Saviour.

**VERSES 14-25: "For we know that the law is spiritual: but I am carnal, sold under sin. For that which I do I allow not: for what I would, that do I not; but what I hate, that do I. If then I do that which I would not, I consent unto the law that it is good. Now then it is no more I that do it, but sin that dwelleth in me. For I know that in me (that is, in my flesh,) dwelleth no good thing: for to will is present with me; but *how* to perform that which is good I find not. For the good that I would I do not: but the evil which I would not, that I do. Now if I do that I would not, it is no more I that do it, but sin that dwelleth in me. I find then a law, that, when I would do good, evil is present with me. For I delight in the law of God after the inward man: But I see another law in my members, warring against the law of my mind, and bringing me into captivity to the law of sin which is in my members. O wretched man that I am! who shall deliver me from the body of this death? I thank God through Jesus Christ our Lord. So then with the mind I myself serve the law of God; but with the flesh the law of sin."**

Verse 14: **"we know that the law is spiritual** [present tense]: **but I am carnal** [present tense]." Here you find the two natures in the believer. Paul wanted to serve the Lord. Paul wanted to keep the law. Why? Because he loved God, he loved the law, he meditated on the law every day. But it was impossible to serve God and keep the law at the same time. That's the Adamic nature. One more time: man is at enmity with God. Man on his own cannot please God. The Lord has to do something for him, that being the Lord Jesus Christ, of course!

Also from verse 14 down to 24, Paul is making it very clear that you cannot serve the Lord while you are born again while at the same time trying to keep the law. It's like being married to a person and trying to please somebody outside of the marriage. Two's company; three's a crowd.

So, Paul has gone from a prosecuting attorney, making it very clear how all have sinned and come short of the glory of God, and those that want to keep the law after they've been saved, are now adulterers. And from them, he has gone on to being a defending attorney, defending the law and defending the Lord Jesus Christ. But, at the same time, realising just how weak he is and vicariously all of us are. So, what does he do? He throws himself at the mercy of the court.

Verse 25, one more time: **"I thank God through Jesus Christ our Lord. So then with the mind I myself serve the law of God; but with the flesh the law of sin." "I thank God through Jesus Christ our Lord."** When man is in dire straits he has to turn to the Lord God of the Bible and say, "God, be merciful to me a sinner. And God saves that sinner the moment he calls on His name. The law condemns you and kills you, but Jesus Christ forgives you and makes you alive.

So, if you, a saved person, tries to keep the law after you have been saved and forgiven and exonerated, you will die. But if you continue on with the Lord Jesus Christ, walking with Him in the Spirit, He will continue to grow you and mature you and to prune you, and you will be victorious in everything that you do for Him. Why? Because He is at the centre of your life and He lives within you, and it is He that makes these things possible. Not you walking in the flesh, but you walking in the Spirit. All glory to God!

# CHAPTER 8

VERSE 1: "*There is* therefore now no condemnation to them which are in Christ Jesus, who walk not after the flesh, but after the Spirit."

No condemnation, no damnation, no judgment to those that are in Christ Jesus, for those that are in God the Father, and for those that are in God the Holy Spirit. And also God the Father and God the Son and God the Holy Spirit are in you as well. The triune God lives within you. Outside of the Trinity, you are the most important person in the world, if you are born again.

Please turn to Psalm 103. Look at verse 12: **"As far as the east is from the west,** *so* **far hath he removed our transgressions from us."** Look at verse 8: **"The LORD** *is* **merciful and gracious, slow to anger, and plenteous in mercy."** Look at verse 10: **"He hath not dealt with us after our sins; nor rewarded us according to our iniquities."**

Please turn back to Romans chapter 8. Look at verse 1 one more time**: "*There is* therefore now** [not in the future, not possibly, not maybe, but "*There is* therefore now"] **no condemnation** [no judgment, no damnation] **to them which are in Christ Jesus,"** and that only occurs once you are born again. The latter part of verse 1**: "who walk not after the flesh, but after the Spirit"** in reference to law and grace.

Chapters 5, 6 and 7 made it very clear that we, the born again children of God, are not under the law. We are married to the Lord Jesus Christ. We are married to grace.

**VERSES 2-9: "For the law of the Spirit of life in Christ Jesus hath made me free from the law of sin and death. For what the law could not do, in that it was weak through the flesh, God sending his own Son in the likeness of sinful flesh, and for sin, condemned sin in the flesh: That the righteousness of the law might be fulfilled in us, who walk not after the flesh, but after the Spirit. For they that are after the flesh do mind the things of the flesh; but they that are after the Spirit the things of the Spirit. For to be carnally minded *is* death; but to be spiritually minded *is* life and peace. Because the carnal mind *is* enmity against God: for it is not subject to the law of God, neither indeed can be. So then they that are in the flesh cannot please God. But ye are not in the flesh, but in the Spirit, if so be that the Spirit of God dwell in you. Now if any man have not the Spirit of Christ, he is none of his."**

Verses 2 down to 9 continue the theme: how we that are born again, how we that are in Christ Jesus are not in the flesh but are in the Spirit, with the flesh representing the law and the Spirit representing grace. Old Covenant and New Covenant. Those that walk in the flesh cannot please God. In fact, they are carnally minded, according to verse 6, and the result of such people is death!

Also from verse 9 Paul says that if any man does not have the Spirit of Christ, he is none of his. No Spirit, no salvation. No salvation, you can't have the mind of Christ. Therefore, you are at enmity against God (verse 7). Why? Because your mind is carnal and as such, it cannot be subject to the law of God. You must be born again, and once you are born again you walk in the Spirit, not in the flesh.

**Chapter 8, verses 10-11: "And if Christ *be* in you, the body *is* dead because of sin; but the Spirit *is* life because of righteousness. But if the Spirit of him that raised up Jesus from the dead dwell in you, he that raised up Christ from the dead shall also quicken your mortal bodies by his Spirit that dwelleth in you."**

In chapter 1, verse 4, we found the Holy Spirit being credited with the resurrection of the Lord Jesus Christ. In Galatians, chapter 1, God the Father resurrected the Lord Jesus Christ. And in John chapter 2, God the Son resurrected Himself. The triune God resurrected the Lord Jesus Christ.

Verse 10: **"if Christ *be* in you, the body *is* dead because of sin"**, meaning the old man is dead with Christ. The old man has been buried with Christ. The old man was identified, was convicted under the law, but Jesus Christ has come and fulfilled the law. **"But the Spirit [meaning grace, meaning the New Covenant] is life because of righteousness"**, found in chapter 10 to be Christ's righteousness. And in the latter part of verse 11: **"he that raised up Christ from the dead shall also quicken your mortal bodies by his Spirit that dwelleth in you."** Not by your works, not by your baptism, not by your church attendance, but by his Spirit. Salvation is of the Lord. The Lord owns everything. He does not need you to do anything for Him when it comes to your salvation. It is a free gift!

**VERSES 12-13: "Therefore, brethren, we are debtors, not to the flesh, to live after the flesh. For if ye live after the flesh, ye shall die: but if ye through the Spirit do mortify the deeds of the body, ye shall live."**

Verse 12: Brethren, brothers, we, all of us, are not debtors to the flesh (one more time, being the law; one more time, being in the Old Covenant) to live after the flesh. Why? Because we have been set free from the Old Covenant! We have been set free from the law!

And he goes on to say in verse 13: **"For if ye** [meaning all of you] **live after the flesh, ye** [all of you] **shall die** [physically, prematurely]: **but if ye** [all of you] **through the [Holy] Spirit** [not your own flesh] **do mortify [put off] the deeds of the body, ye** [all of you] **shall live."**

You're going to die anyway. Ten in ten people die. Saved people die, as do unsaved people die. The only question that needs to be asked is when and why. I will say this also, in reference to verse 13, before I conclude this broadcast, how this also has reference to a saved person walking in the Spirit and living a holy life. To mortify the deeds of the body means don't make provision for sin. Your positional standing with the Lord and your relationship with Him is one thing, but your practical standing with the Lord is something else altogether, and next time we will look at that in some more detail.

So, we are nearly halfway through chapter 8 of the Epistle to the Romans.

And in verses 1 down to 13, Paul has been making the argument very clearly how we are not under the law, but we are under grace. We walk in the Spirit (being the New Covenant), not in the flesh (being the Old Covenant).

Verse 13 ended with an apostolic warning that, for those that live after the flesh, they will die. The wages of sin is death. Not just those that keep the law, meaning they wear skull caps, or they keep Jewish rituals, or they circumcise their sons, or they abstain from foods and meats and meals, or they create additional rituals, rules and regulations, but no! Those that also feed the flesh. Or those that perhaps embrace immorality.

Please turn to Ephesians chapter 6. Look at verse 1: **"Children, obey your parents in the Lord: for this is right. Honour thy father and mother; (which is the first commandment with promise;) That it may be well with thee, and thou mayest live long on the earth."** Saved children obeying their saved parents results in them living long on the earth. Disobedience will result in a premature death. The Lord hates rebellion of any kind, but especially from a child to a parent. He detests it.

Please turn to Acts chapter 5. Look at verse 1: **"But a certain man named Ananias, with Sapphira his wife, sold a possession, And kept back *part* of the price, his wife also being privy *to it*, and brought a certain part, and laid *it* at the apostles' feet. But Peter said, Ananias, why hath Satan filled thine heart to lie to the Holy Ghost, and to keep back** *part* of the price of the land? Whiles it remained, was it not thine own? and after it was sold, was it not in thine own power? why hast thou conceived this thing in thine heart? thou hast not lied unto men, but unto God."

Here we find a saved couple, not only lying to the apostle Peter, but also to the Holy Spirit, found in verse 3 and verse 5, and the Holy Spirit in verse 5 is called God. These two saved people have sinned after the flesh. Their sin was to lie.

Look at verse 5: **"And Ananias hearing these words fell down, and gave up the ghost: and great fear came on all them that heard these things."** Ananias, being the husband and head of the family dies first of all. He takes responsibility first and foremost. He falls first.

Look at verse 9: **"Then Peter said unto her, How is it that ye have agreed together to tempt the Spirit of the Lord? behold, the feet of them which have buried thy husband *are* at the door, and shall carry thee out. Then fell she down straightway at his feet, and yielded up the ghost: and the young men came in, and found her dead, and, carrying *her* forth, buried *her* by her husband."**

Now it's her turn to be judged and found guilty. And she, too, dies just like her husband. Not spiritually, but physically.

**VERSE 14: "For as many as are led by the Spirit of God, they are sons of God."**

Chapter 8, verse 1: "*There is* therefore now no condemnation to them which are in Christ Jesus." Verse 9: "if any man have not the Spirit of Christ, he is none of his."

These three verses all say the same thing. Chapter 8, verse 1, makes it very clear that once you are in Christ Jesus, there is no condemnation for you. Verse 9 makes it even clearer that if you don't have the Spirit, you don't have salvation. And by verse 14, not only are you a Christian (meaning you are a follower of the Lord Jesus Christ), but you are also a son of God. Not just a Bible-believing Christian, but a son of God!

Go back to the Old Testament and look up the term **"sons of God,"** and you find very clearly that it is always in reference in angels! So, we replace the fallen angels back in the Old Testament. We aren't angels, we are still human beings here and now, but when we die, we are like the spirits, we are like the angels. We are going to be sinless. So the next time somebody asks you what you believe, tell them: say you are a Bible-believing Christian and you are also a son of God, you are a son of the Highest. And they will look at you like you have two heads. But it is true. You are a son of God, found very clearly in verse 14.

**VERSE 15: "For ye have not received the spirit of bondage again to fear; but ye have received the Spirit of adoption, whereby we cry, Abba, Father."**

Abba Father means "daddy". Daddy in Aramaic. Can you believe it? Not only are you called a son of God, from verse 14, but now, in verse 15, we can call the Lord of the universe "daddy." This intimacy was unknown prior to the New Covenant.

Please turn to Ephesians chapter 2. Look at verse 12: **"That at the time ye were without Christ, being aliens from the commonwealth of Israel, and strangers from the covenants of promise, having no hope, and without God in the world: But now in Christ Jesus ye who sometimes were far off are made nigh by the blood of Christ."**

Verse 12: aliens and strangers, outside of the commonwealth of Israel. Verse 13: but by the blood of Christ you are now made nigh in Christ Jesus.

He has reconciled you unto him by his own precious blood. Look at verse 14: **"For he is our peace, who hath made both one, and hath broken down the middle wall of partition** *between us***; Having abolished in his flesh the enmity,** *even* **the law of commandments** *contained* **in ordinances; for to make in himself of twain one new man,** *so* **making peace; And that he might reconcile both unto God in one body by the cross, having slain the enmity thereby: And came and preached peace to you which were afar off, and to them that were nigh."** It could not be any clearer. No Jew, no Gentile, no law. He has fulfilled the law and he has destroyed the wall between God and man.

Please turn back to Romans chapter 8. Look at verse 15 a little more closely. **"For ye have not received the spirit of bondage again to fear"**. What fear is he speaking about? Please turn to Hebrews chapter 2. The word of God tells us in 1 John chapter

5 that we can know that we are saved, and we have already seen very clearly from Romans chapter 8, verse 1, how there is no condemnation to those which are in Christ Jesus.

So, what is this fear spoken about in Romans chapter 8? Look at Hebrews chapter 2. Let's start in verse 14: **"Forasmuch then as the children are partakers of flesh and blood, he also himself likewise took part of the same; that through death he might destroy him that had the power of death, that is, the devil; And deliver them who through fear of death were all their lifetime subject to bondage."** That word bondage is found very clearly in verse 15 to be in reference of a) dying and b) in fear of the devil. Death is fearful, but Jesus Christ has abolished death.

Please turn back to Romans chapter 8 and let's look at verse 15 one more time. **"For ye have not received the spirit of bondage again to fear".** Fear of dying. And fear of not keeping the law to perfection. And Paul says, forget it! don't worry! Why? Because **"ye have received the Spirit of adoption, whereby we** [you and I] **cry, Abba, Father."** Like I say, we can call the Lord of the universe "daddy." Why? Because Jesus Christ has knocked down the middle wall [like a barrier or prison] of partition. He has fulfilled the law for us.

Fear of death and fear of coming short of His glory isn't something which should concern you. Rest in Him. He has given you peace. He has the keys. He is the bridge. He is the way, the truth and the life. And He is the only mediator between God and man.

**VERSES 16-17: "The Spirit itself beareth witness with our spirit, that we are the children of God: And if children, then heirs; heirs of God, and joint-heirs with Christ; if so be that we suffer with *him*, that we may be also glorified together."**

From verses 16 down to 39, the apostle Paul is looking way beyond justification and sanctification. Now he is focusing on adoption, something which occurs after you are born again. In verse 14, you are called a son of God, and as such there is no condemnation to those which are in Christ Jesus, found in verse 1. But verse 16 makes the case very clearly how the Holy Spirit bears witness with our spirit how we are the children of God. And not just children, from verse 7, but heirs of God. Joint-heirs with Christ. We are going to rule and reign with the Lord Jesus Christ. We are children of the King, and He is our Father. All that He has, He has given to the Son, and we are going to be joint-heirs with Christ.

And the latter part from verse 17: **"that we may be also glorified together."** Glorification leads into eternity, which simply means you are now going to be sinless, which occurs after you have been adopted.

Pre the new birth (and I showed you from Ephesians chapter 2, how we, before we were born again, were outside of the Commonwealth of Israel). We were orphans, if you will.

But through the new birth, Jew and Gentile are now one in Christ Jesus, Galatians chapter 3. And also in reference to the Holy Spirit testifying with our spirit, how we are the children of God. Not only does He do that through the fruits of the

Spirit: we grow in grace, we love the Lord, and we deny ourselves by picking up our cross and walking and fellowshipping with Him. But also we have it in the Scriptures: **"the Son of Man is come to seek and to save that which was lost"** (Luke 19:10). "All those the Father gives to Me will come to Me... and I shall lose none of those" (John 6:37-39). Salvation is of God, not of man.

**VERSE 18: "For I reckon that the sufferings of this present time *are* not worthy *to be compared* with the glory which shall be revealed in us."**

The latter part of verse 17: if we suffer with Him, we are going to be glorified together with Him. First of all, in reference to your salvation (meaning once you are saved, you will suffer for Him), but also in reference to your testimony, in reference to your practical standing. Once you are saved, you are expected to live a certain way, and the more you deny yourself, and the closer you walk with the Lord, and the greater you suffer for His name's sake, the greater your rewards are going to be in the millennial reign.

But no two saints are the same. The same calling for salvation, but a different calling for service. Found in chapter 9: **"Jacob have I loved, but Esau have I hated."** More on that when we get to chapter 9.

Also, from verse 18, Paul speaks about the sufferings (plural), that they were enduring. It could have been everything: from the Jews putting pressure on believing Jews to go back to the law, to somehow continue on under the Mosaic Covenant, and

Paul condemned that in the earlier chapters. It could also have been in reference to the Gentiles trying to better themselves also, by keeping the law. The Corinthians were also under great pressure to live after the flesh, and Paul says, No, keep on going. Keep your eyes fixed on the Lord Jesus Christ. Don't allow the cares of the world to distract you or to derail your walk with the Lord. Paul is like a father. He loved the churches and he was desperate for them to be faithful to the Lord, to remain in fellowship with the Lord and to shun sin. To be a rebel against sin, but to be a slave to holiness.

**VERSES 19-21: "For the earnest expectation of the creature waiteth for the manifestation of the sons of God. For the creature was made subject to vanity, not willingly, but by reason of him who hath subjected *the same* in hope, Because the creature itself also shall be delivered from the bondage of corruption into the glorious liberty of the children of God."**

Romans chapter 5, Paul made it very clear how Adam's sin has affected all men without exception, and here, all of the animal kingdom are also affected through the sin of Adam. Pre the fall of Adam, all of the animals were vegetarians. Post the fall of Adam, man becomes a meat-eater, animals become meat-eaters. They too have suffered as a result of Adam's sin. One more time, in Adam all men have fallen. In Adam all men have died. In Adam all men are guilty, without exception. But in Christ, all men can be made alive, can be forgiven, can be exonerated, if they believe on Him. **"The just shall live by faith."** But here Paul is looking into eternity, where the animals are going to be able to go back to how they used to be. No more killing, no more suffering, no more survival of the fittest.

**Chapter 8, verse 22: "For we know that the whole creation groaneth and travaileth in pain together until now."**

Adam was made first. Through his sin, the animals have suffered. Like I say, before the fall of Adam, everyone, man and beast, were vegetarian. They lived side by side. But through his fall, that all changed overnight. Mankind is in pain. Mankind is travailing in pain together with the animal kingdom. Even saved people are in great pain. Even saved people are in bondage. Hence, why we looked in some detail at those verses earlier on. And Paul says that the whole of creation is in pain up until now ("now" being the Church age).

Jesus Christ has died for the sins of the world. At a point in the future, when He returns, all of the suffering that mankind and the animal kingdom have experienced will be done away with. Mankind, meaning those that are saved. Animals in general will no longer suffer, as a consequence of Adam, their father's original sin, because he, too, is their corporate father figure.

**VERSE 23: "And not only *they*, but ourselves also, which have the firstfruits of the Spirit, even we ourselves groan within ourselves, waiting for the adoption, *to wit*, the redemption of our body."**

Romans chapter 7, Paul was lamenting his old man clashing with a new man: O wretched man that I am! Who will deliver me from this body? Who will deliver me from this death? I thank Jesus Christ our Lord.

But two points at which to look at very briefly in verse 23: how we, the born-again Bible-believing Christians, have already received the first fruits of the Spirit, being justification and sanctification. And yet we are still awaiting adoption. We are not yet sinless. I showed you that from Romans chapter 7 and Philippians chapter 3. We are still waiting for our new bodies. Paul told you in verse 22 how the whole creation is groaning. That includes saved people and unsaved people. But Paul is primarily interested in the welfare of the Bible-believing Christian. He's saying: It is coming. It will soon be here. Hang in there, but for here and now rest in Him.

**VERSES 24-26: "For we are saved by hope: but hope that is seen is not hope: for what a man seeth, why doth he yet hope for? But if we hope for that we see not, *then* do we with patience wait for *it*. Likewise the Spirit also helpeth our infirmities: for we know not what we should pray for as we ought: but the Spirit itself maketh intercession for us with groanings which cannot be uttered."**

In verse 16, the Holy Spirit confirms that we are the children of God. In verse 26, the Holy Spirit makes intercession for us because we don't know what or how we should pray. We should know, but we don't know. Why? Because we are groaning, we are travailing in pain until now. We still have our fallen natures. So, what a merciful God we have! The Holy Spirit intercedes for us, and God the Son also prays for us.

Also the term **"hope that is not seen".** We don't have a blind faith. Our hope is substantiated on a person, being the Lord

Jesus Christ, and on the Bible – God's 66 books to us, His love letters to us.

Look at verse 27: **"And he that searcheth the hearts knoweth what *is* the mind of the Spirit, because he maketh intercession for the saints according to *the will of* God."**

How does He do this? Because He is God. Found in chapter 1, verse 4. Found in Acts chapter 5. Jesus Christ said He would send another Comforter, being the Holy Spirit, of course. And He prays for us because He is God and He knows what is best for us. Because He is God. Because He loves us.

I just need to make a very quick and a very important footnote, in reference to verse 21, where the word of God tells us: **"Because the creature itself also shall be delivered from the bondage of corruption into the glorious liberty of the children of God."** Jesus Christ did not die for the sins of the animals. Why? Because animals don't have a soul. They have spirits, but they do not have souls.

He died for the sins of the world, and yet by His death, He has redeemed the animal kingdom from the curse of the law. And yet, saying that, please let me say this: their redemption, if you will, does not occur, does not come into place, until the end of the millennial reign. Why? Because during the millennium, animals are going to be sacrificed. So, this piece of Scripture, I believe, has a much futuristic application to it. Yes, they have been redeemed from the curse of the law, but it doesn't come into action until the end of the millennial reign. Only when the eternal state commences are all of the animal kingdom going to get peace from sin, from the fall of Adam.

**VERSE 28: "And we know that all things work together for good to them that love God, to them who are the called according to *his* purpose."**

First of all, the Lord calls all men to repent. Romans chapter 1 verse 16 Paul said it was the power of salvation to everyone that believeth, to the Jew first and also to the Gentile. But here, Paul is primarily focusing on those that have believed the call to repentance, those that have appropriated the atonement. God has made a provision to save mankind, but only those that believe the gospel are going to be saved. If you are not saved, there is no point saying the Lord loves me, He has received me as I am. He has not. He hates all workers of iniquity. He is angry with the wicked every day. He wants you to repent now.

But if you are born again, this verse should be of great comfort to you. Why? Because everything that is good, and everything that is bad when it comes to the life or the daily routine of a Bible-believing Christian happens for a purpose.

But look at verse 28 one more time: **"and we know."** Not just Paul, but all of the apostles knew that all things, everything, without exception, works together for good to them that love God, those that are born again, to them who are the called according to His purpose. Here Paul is looking from the standpoint of the Lord's sovereignty, and the Lord says, If you love Me, everything in your life will work together for good. You will be tempted. You will have trials and tribulations, but hang in there! 1 Corinthians made it very clear that we, the born-again Bible-believing Christians, won't be tempted and won't be tested above what we can endure.

The great Job, from the Old Testament, had trial after trial after trial, but he remained faithful unto the end, and the Lord publicly rewarded him for that. So, if you are saved, if you are going through trials and tribulations, hang in there! Don't give up! And if you are backsliding, repent, confess your sins to Him. These things happen for a reason, but above all, if you are His, He is yours, He will never leave you and He will never forsake you. All things, everything, work together for good to those that love Him.

So just before this broadcast concludes, I need to make a very quick and an important footnote in reference to one word: the word "purpose". **"According to *his* purpose."** What is God's purpose? God has a purpose for everything: a) He wants all men to be saved, and b) He will use all men, whether saved or not, to fulfil His will.

Look at chapter 9 verse 17: **"For the scripture saith unto Pharaoh [it is alive not just a thing], Even for this same purpose have I raised thee up, that I might shew my power in thee, and that my name might be declared throughout all the earth."** It was God's purpose to raise up Pharaoh to achieve His will, that being, of course, the deliverance of Israel and also the destruction of Pharaoh's kingdom.

But chapter 8, verse 28, I believe, has a two-fold meaning: it is God's purpose for man to be saved and it is also God's purpose for certain men, whether saved or not, to serve Him. So, if you read these verses carefully, you will see the difference, many times, between service and salvation. But more in chapter 9 when we get there.

**VERSE 29: "For whom he did foreknow, he also did predestinate *to be* conformed to the image of his Son, that he might be the firstborn among many brethren."**

Calvinists and Armenians have fought over this verse, and also verse 30, for centuries.

So, please join me as I attempt to faithfully dissect verse 29 in minute detail. **"For whom he did foreknow, he also did predestinate *to be* conformed to the image of his Son."** He (being God) foreknew who would believe on the Lord Jesus Christ. And that person that believed on the Lord Jesus Christ was then predestinated to be conformed to the image of His Son. Verse 29 does not tell us when this happened, or even why this happened from the standpoint of God's sovereignty. And I put it to you that you were preordained to be conformed to the image of His Son when you believed on Him. You weren't chosen before the foundation of the world, but you were saved from the beginning of the gospel. You were saved the moment you believed on the call to repent.

John 3:16 is a great piece of Scripture to explain a) God's sovereignty and b) man's free will. **"For God so loved the world, that he gave his only begotten Son, that whosoever believeth in him should not perish, but have everlasting life."** One more time: **"For God so loved the world, that**

**he gave** [that's God's provision, that's God's atonement, that's God's salvation] **his only begotten Son** [the precious and spotless Lamb of God, the only mediator between God and men], **that whosoever believeth in him** [that's man's free will, you can either receive it, or you can reject it] **that whosoever believeth in him should not perish** [meaning go to Hell], **but have** [present tense] **everlasting life."** Exoneration. Salvation. Heaven when you die, not Hell.

So, back to verse 29, one more time: **"For whom he did foreknow, he also did predestinate *to be* conformed to the image of his Son, that he might be the firstborn among many brethren."** Not firstborn in a chronological sense but firstborn in a sense of pre-eminence. And **"to be conformed to the image of his Son"** happens after justification and it happens after sanctification.

So, one quick and final recap, in reference to verse 29: God is sovereign, man is not. God knew through foreknowledge who was going to believe on the Lord Jesus Christ and who would not believe on the Lord Jesus Christ. And I believe the only way to understand verse 29 and verse 30 is through "middle knowledge", and I will get to that in the next broadcast.

**VERSE 30: "Moreover whom he did predestinate, them he also called: and whom he called, them he also justified: and whom he justified, them he also glorified."**

When did this happen and why did this happen? These are the questions that we need to ask ourselves. The Calvinists believe that God has chosen a remnant of people in any given dispensation to be saved, and only those people have been atoned for. They, according to the Calvinists, are the elect. And they, according to the Calvinists, are the only ones that can be saved. Jesus Christ, according to the Calvinists, only died for those people. And they believe they were chosen in Christ Jesus before the foundation of the world.

So, let's examine verse 30 in a little more fine detail. **"Moreover whom he did predestinate, them he also called: and whom he called, them he also justified: and whom he justified, them he also glorified."** And why did God predestinate those people to be conformed to the image of his Son? Because through foreknowledge and middle knowledge, He knew who was going to believe on his Son.

The Old Testament prophets were chosen in time to write what they wrote. And what they saw happening in the future, they wrote down. Nobody made person A, B or C do something which was against their will. The Lord knew how person A, B and C would respond in any given situation. And the same is true of salvation. God has always known through foreknowledge and middle knowledge those that were going to believe on the Lord Jesus Christ. Nobody was forced or coerced to believe on the Lord Jesus Christ. Man has a free will. He can either receive the Lord Jesus Christ or he can reject the Lord Jesus Christ. And so here, I believe, in verse 30, Paul is looking at the atonement from the standpoint of the Lord's sovereignty, from the standpoint of God's foreknowledge.

John 3:16, one more time: **"For God so loved the world** [everyone and everything!] **that he gave** [gift] **his only**

**begotten Son** [the Lamb of God, the sinless Saviour, the only Mediator between man and God] **that whosoever** [Jew or Gentile, Romans 1:16] **believeth in him** [no works] should not perish [suffer in Hell] for ever], **but have everlasting life** [present tense]." God is sovereign. Man has a free will. The two run side by side. We cannot understand these things, but we are told to believe these things.

So, based on foreknowledge and middle knowledge, the moment a person in time believes on the Lord Jesus Christ, they are predestinated in the mind of the Lord before the foundation of the world – because God is sovereign – to be conformed to the image of His Son. But before that occurs, they have to be called in time. Called to repent. And once they've been called to repent, and once they have repented, then they are justified in time, not before the foundation of the world. And once they have been justified, then they are glorified, which here comes after sanctification. You see, here Paul is looking beyond time. Paul wrote this around 56 A.D. and here he is looking into eternity. Glorification comes after sanctification and it comes once a person has been adopted into the family of God.

So, at this point in our study of the Epistle to the Romans, we have arrived at the halfway mark. Halfway through chapter 8 and halfway through the Epistle to the Romans. Paul was a genius, and chapter 8 is a masterpiece. Only the apostle Paul could explain the sovereignty of the Lord God of the Bible and the free will of man. So for this broadcast please join me as I return to verses 28, 29 and 30, and let's see what additional light we can ascertain from these verses.

Verse 28: **"And we know that all things work together for good to them that love God, to them who are the called according to *his* purpose."** This verse proves conclusively that the Lord God of the Bible is all-powerful. He has to be all-powerful in order to make every single event in the life of a born-again Bible-believer come to pass in a good way. Temporarily, it could be a troublesome time. Temporarily, you could be under great distress and pressure, but ultimately, good will come from it.

If you go back to the Book of Genesis, you discover Joseph being sold into slavery by his own brethren, and chapter 50 says, you [meaning Joseph's brothers] meant it for evil, but God meant it for good. Temporarily, Joseph was sold into slavery. He could have died in prison. But the Lord had a plan for Joseph because Joseph was greatly beloved. As was Daniel.

So, verse 28 says, one more time, **"we know that all things** [everything, without exception, good and bad] **work together for good to them that love God, to them who are the called according to *his* purpose."** He calls all men to repent, but only those that believe on the Lord Jesus Christ are going to be saved. But like I say, one more time, the Lord can and does use unsaved people to achieve His purpose.

But in reference to what occurred back in Genesis, with the brothers of Joseph sending him into slavery, they did that through their own free will. The Lord God of the Bible did not preordain that to occur before the foundation of the world. He allowed it to happen, and from their evil and their free will, the Lord God of the Bible was able to use that for His ultimate good. So, when we go back to Genesis chapter 50, we discover how the Lord God of the Bible allowed Joseph's brethren to do what they did. He did not preordain that to happen before the foundation of the world, although He knew it would happen before the foundation of the world, but He allowed his brothers to do what they did in time, and through their sin, through their evil, the Lord allowed good to come from that.

Middle knowledge, I believe, is the only way to understand the sovereignty of the Lord and the free will of man. Nobody made Joseph's brothers do what they did. They did what they did because they were wicked, but the Lord God one more time took their evil and made it into good, and the same is true of us. Before we were saved, we did wicked and evil things, and yet through our wickedness, the Lord God has used that to bring us to Him.

**VERSES 29-30: "For whom he did foreknow, he also did predestinate *to be* conformed to the image of his Son, that he might be the firstborn among many brethren. Moreover whom he did predestinate, them he also called: and whom he called, them he also justified: and whom he justified, them he also glorified."** This is the source of the new birth, not the reason for the new birth.

**VERSE 29: "For whom he did foreknow."** He knows everyone and He knows everything, from the beginning of creation, from eternity past into eternity future. But here Paul is looking at those that are going to be saved. The only question that we need to ask is why are they going to be saved and how are they going to be saved and when were they predestinated to be conformed to the image of His Son?

Please turn to Jeremiah chapter 1. Look at verse 4: **"Then the word of the LORD came unto me, saying, Before I formed thee in the belly I knew thee; and before thou camest forth out of the womb I sanctified thee, *and* I ordained thee a prophet unto the nations."** Before Jeremiah was even born, he was known in the mind of the Lord. But so too was Pharaoh, and Herod, and Caiaphas. The only difference here is that Jeremiah was chosen through middle knowledge to be a prophet unto the nations. The Lord God knew before the foundation of the world that Jeremiah would believe on Him, whereas Pharaoh and Herod and Caiaphas would not.

Please go back to Romans chapter 8, verse 29, one more time: **"For whom he did foreknow, he also did predestinate *to be* conformed to the image of his Son."** You were chosen and predestinated to be conformed to the image of His Son the moment you believed on the Lord Jesus Christ, and these are the people that responded to the call to salvation. These people responded to the call to repentance, and then they were justified, and then they were glorified.

So Paul, with the mind of Christ, living in time, is looking at verses 28 and 29 and 30 from eternity past into eternity future, from the standpoint of what the Lord knows, not what we know. And he is explaining to us that those that have appropriated the atonement are the called and these people are then predestinated to be conformed to the image of Jesus Christ. All done in time, as far as we the sinners are concerned.

But as far as the Lord is concerned, and I showed you from Jeremiah chapter 1, these things happened before we were even born!

**VERSE 31: "What shall we then say to these things? If God *be* for us, who *can be* against us?"**

Once you are born again, you are forever safe. So, one more time: just rest in Him!

**VERSE 32: "He that spared not his own Son, but delivered him up for us all, how shall he not with him also freely give us all things?"**

This is in reference to adoption. We are co-heirs with God, we are joint-heirs with Christ.

**VERSE 33: "Who shall lay any thing to the charge of God's elect? *It is* God that justifieth."**

Once you are born again, no one and nothing can come against you. You are safe in Him. You belong to Him and He belongs to you.

**VERSE 34: "Who *is* he that condemneth? *It is* Christ that died, yea rather, that is risen again, who is even at the right hand of God, who also maketh intercession for us."**

The devil will seek to destroy you and he will seek to rob you of your assurance in Jesus Christ, but Jesus is at the right hand of God making intercession for you to the Father. You can't be touched! Outside of the triune God, you are the most important person in the world. And outside of the triune God, you are the safest person. Why? Because you belong to the Lord.

**VERSE 35-39: "Who shall separate us from the love of Christ?** *shall* **tribulation, or distress, or persecution, or famine, or nakedness, or peril, or sword? As it is written, For thy sake we are killed all the day long; we are accounted as sheep for the slaughter. Nay, in all these things we are more than conquerors through him that loved us. For I am persuaded, that neither death, nor life, nor angels, nor principalities, nor powers, nor things present, nor things to come, Nor height, nor depth, nor any other creature, shall be able to separate us from the love of God, which is in Christ Jesus our Lord."**

Romans chapter 8 started in verse 1 with there being no condemnation, no judgment, no damnation, to those that are in Christ Jesus. Verses 35, 36, 37, 38 and 39 make it very clear that no one and nothing can separate you from the love of God. You can't lose your salvation. Tribulation won't do it. Distress won't do it. Persecution won't do it. Famine won't do it. Nakedness won't do it. Peril won't do it. The sword cannot do it. Death can't destroy you. Life cannot rob you. Angels cannot interfere with you. Principalities (meaning fallen angels) cannot take you away from the Lord God of the Bible. They cannot cause you to lose your salvation. Nor powers! It could be here, it could be in the afterlife. No one or nothing can separate you. Nothing or no one can come between you and the Lord!

So, chapter 8 started with there being no condemnation, no judgment, no damnation, to those which are in Christ Jesus. And chapter 8, verse 39 ends, one more time: **"Nor height, nor depth, nor any other creature, shall be able to separate us from the love of God, which is in Christ Jesus our Lord."** We are in Him, and He is in us! We are forever saved. So, eternal security could not be displayed any clearer than what we found in Romans chapter 8.

# CHAPTER 9

<br>

VERSES 1-2: "I say the truth in Christ, I lie not, my conscience also bearing me witness in the Holy Ghost, That I have great heaviness and continual sorrow in my heart."

The Scripture says to rejoice in the Lord always, and yet here Paul says that his conscience bears witness in the Holy Spirit that he has great heaviness for Israel and a continual sorrow.

Paul was lamenting the problem of Israel, for the most part, not believing in the Lord Jesus Christ. Paul loved Israel. Paul was a Jew of the Jews. And clearly, by the statement found in verse 1, one more time: **"I lie not, my conscience also bearing me witness in the Holy Ghost,"** that what Paul is telling us is a reflection of God's view, of God's feeling, of God's grief for the fact that the Jews, for the most part, did not believe and did not receive the message of the Lord Jesus Christ. And yet the same was true of the Old Testament prophets. For the most part, the people of Israel did not believe and did not receive their messages, their warnings, either!

So it's clear to me that verses 1 and verses 2 are a clear apostolic reflection of the Lord's will that He wanted Israel to be saved. He did not chose a group of people before the foundation of the world to be saved, and the rest were left to be damned. No, that's not what the Scripture tells us. Paul says one more time: **"I lie not, my conscience also bearing me witness in** the Holy Ghost, 2 That I have great heaviness and continual sorrow in my heart."

The apostle Paul had the mind of Christ. The apostle Paul went to the third Heaven, and the apostle Paul wrote most of the New Testament. If he did not know the mind of the Lord, I put it to you that nobody knows the mind of the Lord. Yes, through the foreknowledge of the Lord, the Lord always knew those that were going to believe on the Lord Jesus Christ and those that would not believe on the Lord Jesus Christ.

The same is true of the Old Testament prophets that were sent many times to preach to backslidden and apostate Israel. The Lord always knew which Jews would believe their message to repent, and which Jews would not believe their message to repent.

But here Paul is writing the Epistle to the Romans, 56 A.D., having to try and understand and reflect the free will of man and the sovereignty of the Lord. Like I say, just because the Lord can see from eternity past into eternity future those that are going to believe on His Son, and those that are not going to believe on His Son, it doesn't negate man's responsibility to believe on the Lord Jesus Christ, and it still grieves the Lord when mankind refuses to bend the knee and instead snubs the Lord Jesus Christ, blasphemes the Lord Jesus Christ.

So, yes, rejoice in the Lord always if you are saved. Romans chapter 8 made it very clear that all things work together for good to them that love God. And yet at the same time, you can mourn, you can grieve over unsaved family and friends. Here, the apostle Paul is doing it for the nation of Israel, and you can do it, and I can do it when it comes to unsaved family and friends. The Lord understands this perfectly well.

**VERSES 3-5: "For I could wish that myself were accursed from Christ for my brethren, my kinsmen according to the flesh: Who are Israelites; to whom *pertaineth* the adoption, and the glory, and the covenants, and the giving of the law, and the service of *God*, and the promises; Whose *are* the fathers, and of whom as concerning the flesh Christ *came*, who is over all, God blessed for ever. Amen."**

**"Christ *came*, who is over all, God blessed for ever, Amen."** El Gibbor. Isaiah chapter 9. Emmanuel: God with us. This verse is a very clear affirmation of the deity, of the divinity, of the Lord Jesus Christ. **"Christ *came*, who is over all, God blessed for ever. Amen."** At the name of Jesus, every knee will bend and every tongue will confess that Christ Jesus is Lord, meaning God.

But go back to verse 3, please: **"For I could wish that myself were accursed from Christ for my brethren, my kinsmen according to the flesh:"** He wants to be cursed! He is prepared to be damned for the sake of Israel!

Please turn to Exodus chapter 32. Which other famous leader was prepared to be damned? Was prepared to be separated from God if it meant Israel could be saved? Look at verse 32, please: **"Yet now, if thou wilt forgive their sin–; and if not, blot me, I pray thee, out of thy book which thou hast written."**

Moses, like the apostle Paul, like Gideon, like Elijah, was prepared to be damned if it meant Israel could be saved. Moses is a type of the Lord Jesus Christ, and many of the Jews left Egypt, which is a type of the world. Most of the Jews did not go into the Promised Land, which is a type of the millennial reign.

But here I am focusing primarily on the man Moses, on the man Paul. Two great Jewish leaders and they were both prepared to be damned! They were both prepared to be accursed from God for the sake of Israel, and both are types clearly of the Lord Jesus Christ.

Please go back to Romans chapter 9. Look at verse 4, please, one more time. How the Israelites, the Jews, the chosen race had pertained to the adoption and the glory and the covenants and the giving of the law and the service of God and the promises, and how they are related to their fathers, the patriarchs. And yet all of this made no difference. Why? Because they would not receive the Lord Jesus Christ–Romans chapter 10, and we will get there shortly.

And he concludes verse 5 one more time: **"Christ *came*, who is over all, God blessed for ever. Amen".** El Gibbor–the mighty God. Elohim–Jehovah God. And yet they would not receive Almighty God as their Messiah and Saviour. And therefore they are not going to be saved, but cast away.

**VERSES 6-8: "Not as though the word of God hath taken none effect. For they *are* not all Israel, which are of Israel: Neither, because they are the seed of Abraham, *are they* all children: but, In Isaac shall thy seed be called. That is,**

**They which are the children of the flesh, these *are* not the children of God: but the children of the promise are counted for the seed."**

Verses 6 down to 8 make it very clear. That not all of Israel is Israel. Like I say, Moses took the children out of Egypt, Egypt being a type of the world. And yet only a few of the Jews that left Egypt went into the Promised Land. They were all physical and literal descendants of Abraham, Isaac and Jacob, and yet only the true and genuine believing Jews went into the Promised Land. Yes, they were children of their forefathers, beloved for the sake of their forefathers, but only a few went into the Promised Land. And Paul says in verse 8, one more time: **"They which are the children of the flesh, these *are* not the children of God: but the children of the promise are counted for the seed."**

You may be a Jew living in the Middle East, you may be a Jew living in Israel, or anywhere in the world, for that matter. You may be a physical descendant of Abraham, Isaac and Jacob, but that does not make you a spiritual or a completed Jew. That, and that alone, won't save you. You must be born again. And of course verses 6 down to 8 and beyond are looking at the coming Messiah.

**VERSES 9-12: "For this *is* the word of promise, At this time will I come, and Sara shall have a son. And not only *this*; but when Rebecca also had conceived by one, *even* by our father Isaac; (For *the children* being not yet born, neither having done any good or evil, that the purpose of God according to**

**election might stand, not of works, but of him that calleth;) It was said unto her, The elder shall serve the younger."**

Look at chapter 8 verse 28, please, one more time: **"And we know that all things work together for good to them that love God, to them who are the called according to *his* purpose."** His purpose, like I say, one more time, is to save people; and for saved people, and sometimes unsaved people, to go on and serve Him. And here we see from verses 9 down to 12, from chapter 9, how the children born to Rebecca hadn't done anything good or evil, and yet due to the purpose of God, due to His election, He chose one above the other, not for salvation but for service.

And also from verse 12, as a quick footnote, the elder normally was the most important person in the family, when it came to the children of course. The elder had a position of authority and pre-eminence, so for the oldest child to serve the youngest child was unheard of. But go back to the Book of Genesis, Cain was the oldest and he fell. Abel was a good man who was put to death prematurely by his older brother.

But returning to Romans chapter 9, with the main theme of the older brother serving the younger brother decided by the Lord God of the Bible with the understanding of foreknowledge, knowing how both brothers would handle any given situation, and yet by the Lord's omniscience, omnipresence and omnipotence He decided that the older brother would serve the younger brother. That is the Lord's prerogative. This is the Lord's universe, He sets the rules and if you don't like it, go and find another universe and we will come along and judge your standards.

But here, Paul makes it very clear, as only he could do, how the Lord is sovereign and man is not, and also very quickly and very importantly I must comment on verse 9: **"At this time will I come, and Sara shall have a son",** being Isaac, of course, found in verse 10. The Messiah came from Isaac. Never mind Ishmael and Hagar which the Muslims claim to be their forefathers, or kinsmen, if you will. The covenant, the seed, the promise was to Isaac, and from Isaac comes the Lord Jesus Christ.

So, during the last broadcast we looked at verses 9 down to 12, in reference to Isaac and Jacob. And verse 11 made it very clear that the purpose of God according to election might stand, not of works, meaning these two had done nothing in order for the Lord to choose one over the other. They weren't even born! **"But of him** [God] **that calleth."** Because He knows everything. He knows the beginning from the end, and He knows which person is better going to serve Him. Never mind what mankind thinks or does! Only the Lord God of the Bible knows man inside out.

And during a previous broadcast I showed you from 1 Samuel how man looks on the outward appearance, but God looks on the inward appearance. The Lord God looks at the heart of man, whereas mankind looks at man's outward works.

So, trust in the Lord! Just allow the Lord to be the Lord. Never mind what you think, never mind what you've been taught or what system or church or background you have come from.

Trust in the Lord! Like I say, He made mankind, He wrote the manual for mankind. He knows perfectly well how His creation works. Trust Him, not man.

Look at verse 13, please:

**VERSE 13: "As it is written, Jacob have I loved, but Esau have I hated."**

Please turn to Malachi, chapter 1. Is God really speaking about two little boys, hating one and loving the other? Look at verse 2, please. **"I have loved you, saith the LORD. Yet ye say, Wherein hast thou loved us?** *Was* **not Esau Jacob's brother? saith the LORD: yet I loved Jacob, And I hated Esau, and laid his mountains and his heritage waste for the dragons of the wilderness."**

So we can see here, very clearly, how Jacob *per se* and Esau *per se* are not the subject of the Lord's love or even his hatred, but their descendants. Jacob is Israel and Esau is Edom, Israel's archenemy, and from Edom came Ishmael, and from Ishmael came Muhammad. So when the Scripture saith, **"Jacob have I loved, and Esau have I hated,"** I believe it is in reference to Israel being loved and Islam being hated. I also believe it is a clear prophecy of things to come. And also, please appreciate how Malachi was written hundreds of years after Jacob and Esau had died.

So during the last broadcast, we looked at Jacob and Esau, two boys, two children chosen in the mind of the Lord before the foundation of the world to serve Him in two very different ways, and yet Malachi explained this to us by writing this in time and after Jacob and Esau had lived and died.

And so Paul, anticipating a potential backlash to this, and also wanting to explain to the Romans how the Lord's sovereignty works, and election in general, tells us the following in verse 14: **"What shall we say then?** *Is there* **unrighteousness with God? God forbid."**

May it never be! Paul takes the position here, once again, as a defence attorney. He anticipates this kind of thinking that perhaps the Lord is unrighteous, and yet the Scripture tells us that God "cannot behold evil" (Habakkuk 1:13). He hates all workers of iniquity. He takes no pleasure in the death of the wicked.

And Paul says here, one more time: **"Is there unrighteousness with God? God forbid."** It is impossible! God is pure, God is sinless, God is holy. But as Abraham, the great patriarch of the Old Testament said in Genesis 18, verse 25: **"Shall not the Judge of all the earth do right?"** Absolutely. This is His world and this is His universe. He is God and we are His subjects, and if we are born again, we are His children, co-heirs with Him, co-heirs with Christ.

Okay, so at this point we are halfway through chapter 9 of the Epistle to the Romans, and chapter 9, like chapter 8, is a very deep and a very controversial and a very misunderstood piece of Scripture. In chapter 9 we discover the word "election," and when you think of the word "election" or the subject of "election," you think of one of two views. The first view would be that of the Calvinists, which believe that the Lord has chosen person A, B and C before the foundation of the world to be saved, and person D, E and F was chosen before the foundation of the world to be damned. And I've already shown you from chapter 8 (and we'll look at chapter 9 shortly, the latter verses, of course) how that is not the case.

But last time we ended on verse 14, where the apostle Paul asks the rhetorical question ***"Is there* any unrighteousness with God?"** and he goes on to say **"God forbid."** The Lord is holy. The Lord cannot behold evil.

But one quick footnote I want to quickly cover, where we discovered in verses 10, 11 and 12, how Rebecca's two sons, Jacob and Esau, not yet being born, had already been chosen for service. And chapter 8, verse 28, one more time, says: **"And we know that all things work together for good to them that love God, to them who are the called according to *his* purpose."** Rebecca loved the Lord, and as a result of loving the Lord, He allowed her to bear two sons: Jacob, of course, went on to be Israel, and from Israel the Messiah came. Esau went on to become an Edomite, and here you find two very powerful kingdoms: the children of Israel and the children of the Edomites. And I showed you last time how Jacob became Israel, **"Israel have I loved,"** and how Esau not only became an Edomite, but from the Edomites came the Ishmaelites, and from the Ishmaelites came the Mohammedans-the Muslims! So "Israel have I loved, Islam have I hated."

But chapter 8, verse 28, demonstrates to me very clearly how Rebecca loved the Lord. She was a saved woman, and therefore

He, the Lord God, used her love, her faith, for Him and in Him to produce two sons. Service and salvation, one more time, are not the same thing. Jacob was called for service, and I believe he was also saved, whereas Esau was called for service but I do not believe he was saved. Hebrews chapter 11 speaks about Esau very clearly. So, just some opening and important thoughts in reference to the sovereignty of the Lord and how He, God, works all things together for good to those that love God. Rebecca and Isaac, being two people that were plucked out by the Lord God to allow great things to come from them. Abraham told Isaac that his seed would be blessed, and Isaac no doubt told Rebecca. Whether or not she fully understood it, or not, we are not told. But nevertheless, through faith she had two sons, one produced Israel and the other produced the Edomites.

**VERSES 15-16: "For he saith to Moses, I will have mercy on whom I will have mercy, and I will have compassion on whom I will have compassion. So then *it is* not of him that willeth, nor of him that runneth, but of God that sheweth mercy."**

Please turn to John chapter 1. Look at verse 11, please. **"He came unto his own, and his own received him not. But as many as received him, to them gave he power to become the sons of God, *even* to them that believe on his name: Which were born, not of blood, nor of the will of the flesh, nor of the will of man, but of God."** Here we find the source of the new birth.

Please go back to Romans chapter 9. It's the same thing. The source of the Lord's will, the source of the Lord's election. Not the reason for election, but the source of election. Romans chapter 9, please. Verse 15, one more time: **"I will have mercy on whom I will have mercy, and I will have compassion on whom I will have compassion."** The Lord withdrew His mercy from King Saul, but not from King Solomon, with Saul dying prematurely, whereas Solomon living to a good old age. Why? Because Solomon was a son of David, the King of Israel, and from David, and from Solomon, would come the Lord Jesus Christ. Saul was cursed and Saul died prematurely. Did he die and go to Hell? No, I don't believe so. But he died prematurely because the Lord withdrew His mercy and His compassion from him.

**Chapter 9, verses 17-22: "For the scripture saith unto Pharaoh, Even for this same purpose have I raised thee up, that I might shew my power in thee, and that my name might be declared throughout all the earth. Therefore hath he mercy on whom he will *have mercy*, and whom he will he hardeneth. Thou wilt say then unto me, Why doth he yet find fault? For who hath resisted his will? Nay but, O man, who art thou that repliest against God? Shall the thing formed say to him that formed *it*, Why hast thou made me thus? Hath not the potter power over the clay, of the same lump to make one vessel unto honour, and another unto dishonour?"**

Yes, of course. The Lord God is sovereign. This is His universe. He can do with us whatever He chooses to do. Man was made from the clay of the ground, and man, according to Revelation chapter 4, was made for the glory of God.

But go back to verse 17, in reference to Pharaoh: **"Even for this same purpose have I raised thee up, that I might shew my power in thee, and that my name might be declared throughout all the earth."** Romans chapter 8. God's purpose here is found in Pharaoh. Pharaoh was a pagan. The Lord God always knew that Pharaoh was going to be a pagan. He was never going to be saved. And so, God, through foreknowledge and middle knowledge, used the sin of Pharaoh for His glory.

Verse 18, one more time: **"Therefore hath he mercy on whom he will *have mercy*, and whom he will he hardeneth."** That's God's prerogative.

And verse 19, Paul understands the response that is going to come from the Romans, and he answers: **"Thou wilt say then unto me, Why doth he yet find fault? For who hath resisted his will?"** It's a fair question. How can God condemn man, when man is doing what God wants him to do? But it's not as simple as that. So, if we take Pharaoh for an example, we find God hardens Pharaoh's heart, and yet at other times Pharaoh hardens his own heart. So, God, through foreknowledge, and God, through middle knowledge, uses Pharaoh to fulfil His will, but Pharaoh was always going to be against God from eternity past. God did not choose him to be against God from eternity past, but God allowed Pharaoh in time, through his own free will, to choose his own way. To choose his own life. To be the person that he was. And the Lord God used that man, Pharaoh, to fulfil His will. Therefore, Pharaoh's will was never violated. So, the Lord God, as the Potter, having power and authority over the clay, took Pharaoh, raised him up, and then destroyed him.

Genesis chapter 50, one more time: You meant it for evil, but I meant it for good. The sovereignty of the Lord, one more time, and the free will of man, one more time, work hand in hand. And many times, the clay is totally unaware as to what is occurring. John chapter 11 is a good example.

Caiaphas was the high priest of the Lord, and yet he did not understand, he did not appreciate the words which came out of his mouth, in reference to the Lord Jesus Christ dying not just for the sins of Israel, but for the sins of the world.

So, during the last broadcast we discovered how the Lord God of the Bible allows saved people and unsaved people to serve Him and to reflect His will and glory many times with them not even realising it. And again, this is the Lord's prerogative. This is His universe. He made the rules. He sets the agenda. We are His subjects, pure and simple.

But for this broadcast I want to start at verse 21 and read it one more time, because 21 feeds into 22 which feeds into 23, which feeds into 24:**"Hath not the potter power over the clay, of the same lump to make one vessel unto honour, and another unto dishonour?** *What* **if God, willing to shew** *his* **wrath, and to make his power known, endured with much longsuffering the vessels of wrath fitted to destruction: And that he might make known the riches of his glory on the vessels of mercy, which he had afore prepared unto glory,**

**Even us, whom he hath called, not of the Jews only, but also of the Gentiles?"**

There is nothing from verses 21 down to 24 to give us any indication that these people (the vessels fitted for honour or the vessels fitted for dishonour) were preordained to do so before the foundation of the world. No! These people were born in time, and some produced fruit and some did not. Some would believe on the Lord Jesus Christ and some would not. And verse 22 is the key to understanding verses 21, 23 and 24. Verse 22, one more time: **"*What* if God, willing to shew *his* wrath, and to make his power known, endured with much longsuffering the vessels of wrath fitted to destruction: And that he might make known the riches of his glory on the vessels of mercy, which he had afore prepared unto glory, Even us, whom he hath called, not of the Jews only, but also of the Gentiles?"**

Verse 22: **"with much longsuffering"**. The Lord is not willing that any should perish but that all should come to repentance. The last verse found in chapter 10: **"But to Israel he saith, All day long I have stretched forth my hands unto a disobedient and gainsaying people."** Why would He bother to do this if He had chosen persons A, B and C before the foundation of the world to be saved, knowing that everyone else was going to go to Hell because He had decided that would be the case? It makes no sense.

So, as far as I am concerned, foreknowledge and middle knowledge is the only way to make sense of these deep issues. The Lord looks from eternity past into eternity future and He sees those living in time: which ones are going to believe on the Lord Jesus Christ and which ones are not going to believe on the Lord Jesus Christ. But either way, He gets the glory. It's all about God, not man.

So, before I start in verse 25, which will take me down to 33 and complete this broadcast, in verse 24 the apostle Paul told us, one more time: **"Even us, whom he hath called, not of the Jews only, but also of the Gentiles?"** He was always going to call the Gentiles. The Lord is the Lord of the Jews and also of the Gentiles. The Jews were His vehicle for the Old Covenant, and it was down to them to reflect the majesty and the love and the reverence of the Lord God of the Bible to their Gentile neighbours.

And I showed you how Mordecai and Esther did that back in the Old Testament. But the Jews failed. They failed on a mass scale. The Old Testament prophets told us that the Jews, for the most part, would not believe and not trust and not follow their leaders. They rejected the Lord God of the Bible. And through their fall, we, the Gentiles, are grafted in. So the call here found in verse 24 is not just for the Jews only, to believe on the Lord Jesus Christ, but also on the Gentiles, and we discovered also from John chapter 10, when the Lord Jesus Christ told us how He had sheep that were not of His fold, meaning the Gentiles. And by His death, burial and resurrection, and subsequent ascension back to Heaven, the Gentiles are also given the opportunity to be saved. Found here, I believe in verse 24, and also in the latter verses of 25 and 26.

So for this broadcast, let's start, please, in verse 25: **"As he saith also in Osee, I will call them my people, which were not my people; and her beloved, which was not beloved."**

Osee being Hosea. **"I will call them my people, which were not my people",** in reference to the Jews, primarily. Some of the Jews believed, some of the Jews did not believe. The Jews that came out of Exodus, the Jews that came out of Egypt, were a mixed multitude. Some believed and some did not. But beyond this, I believe, one more time, is in reference to the Gentiles, the Church.

**VERSE 26: "And it shall come to pass, *that* in the place where it was said unto them, Ye *are* not my people; there shall they be called the children of the living God."**

John chapter 1, verse 11, one more time: **"He came unto his own** [being the Jews] **and his own** [the Jews] **received him not. But as many as received him, to them gave he power to become the sons of God, *even* to them that believe on his name."** So we, the Church, have replaced unbelieving Israel. We are the children of God. We are the people of God. Foretold in the Old Testament and fulfilled at the death, burial and resurrection of the Lord Jesus Christ. But God has not forsaken (permanently) the people of Israel. More on that when we get to chapter 11.

**Chapter 9, verses 27-28: "Esaias also crieth concerning Israel, Though the number of the children of Israel be as the sand of the sea, a remnant shall be saved: For he will finish**

the work, and cut *it* short in righteousness: because a short work will the Lord make upon the earth."

Verse 28 could be in reference to the short life of the Lord Jesus Christ, that being only 33 years old. Also from 27, Esaias is Isaiah.

But look at 29, please: **"And as Esaias said before, Except the Lord of Sabaoth had left us a seed, we had been as Sodoma, and been made like unto Gomorrha."**

Sodom and Gomorrah were destroyed, for their sin of immorality, wickedness, lasciviousness. Israel too (if it hadn't been for the election of God) could also have been destroyed. For they, too, were wicked. They also committed sins of immorality and they also sacrificed their own children to pagan gods. And because of the Lord's mercy and Israel's faithful remnant found in verse 27, and the subsequent seed found in verse 29, Israel was spared, the seed being Isaac, the seed being Jacob, and the seed ultimately being the Lord Jesus Christ. The Lord's mercy is amazing! His majesty is magnificent! The just shall live by faith. Israel was saved by faith. I was saved by faith. And you, if you are saved, were saved by faith. And verses 30 down to 33 explain to us why Israel was not saved on a mass scale, but more on that in the next broadcast.

**VERSES 30-33: "What shall we say then? That the Gentiles, which followed not after righteousness, have attained to righteousness, even the righteousness which is of faith. But Israel, which followed after the law of righteousness, hath not attained to the law of**

righteousness. Wherefore? Because *they sought it* not by faith, but as it were by the works of the law. For they stumbled at that stumblingstone; As it is written. Behold, I lay in Sion a stumblingstone and rock of offence: and whosoever believeth on him shall not be ashamed."

Faith alone. We saw it in chapter 1 verse 16: **"for it is the power of God unto salvation to every one that believeth; to the Jew first, and also to the Greek."** But the Jews wanted to be saved by their works, not by their faith in the finished work of the Lord Jesus Christ! Israel wanted to remain under the Old Covenant. And we looked at that in chapter 7. And that won't save you. And finally the term for **"stumblingstone"** and **"rock of offence"** found in verses 32 and 33 are in reference to the Lord Jesus Christ. He is our Rock. Not Peter, found in Matthew chapter 16, but the Lord Jesus Christ. He, and He alone, is the mediator between God and man. And verse 33 ends, one more time: **"and whosoever** [Jew or Gentile] **believeth on him** [we walk by faith not sight] **shall not be ashamed."** You won't die in your sins, but you will have everlasting life. One more time: it's all about God!

Revelation chapter 4 we find the following in verse 11: **"Thou art worthy, O Lord, to receive glory and honour and power: for thou hast created all things, and for thy pleasure they are and were created."**

So, if you are not saved, and you want to be saved, just call out to the Lord God and say, **"God, be merciful to me, a sinner!"** He is the Just One (meaning without sin) and we are the unjust ones (meaning we are sinful), but He and He alone will bring us to God. One more time: the just shall live by faith!

# CHAPTER 10

VERSES 1-4: "Brethren, my heart's desire and prayer to God for Israel is, that they might be saved. For I bear them record that they have a zeal of God, but not according to knowledge. For they being ignorant of God's righteousness, and going about to establish their own righteousness, have not submitted themselves unto the righteousness of God. For Christ *is* the end of the law for righteousness to every one that believeth."

Chapter 10 is very much in conclusion to chapter 9, where the apostle Paul says how he wished he was accursed if it meant Israel could be saved. And here he starts in chapter 10 with his heart very much on his sleeve. **"Brethren [brothers and sisters], my heart's desire and prayer to God for Israel is, that they might be saved."** The will of the Lord is for all men to be saved, not just the elect, but all men to be saved.

And he goes on to say in verse 2 how they have a zeal of God but not according to knowledge. Knowledge of God. Knowledge of the Lord Jesus Christ. A zeal is all very well, but a zeal without faith – a zeal without faith in the Lord Jesus Christ – is worthless. And he tells us very plainly how Israel is very ignorant of God's righteousness, meaning the imputation of Christ's righteousness, His goodness, His sinlessness. The just shall live by faith. They were ignorant of what the Lord Jesus Christ achieved on the cross. And so what do they do?

They go about to establish their own righteousness. Faith in works. Their deeds and their beads.

And the latter part of verse 3: **"they** [Israel]... **have not submitted themselves unto the righteousness of God",** being the Lord Jesus Christ, of course! Get down on your knees. You cannot save yourself, and He does not need you to help Him to save yourself. He owns everything. And just in case verses 1, 2 and 3 were not clear enough, he tells us in verse 4: **"For Christ** [the Messiah, the Chosen One, the Just One] *is* **the end of the law for righteousness to every one that believeth."** Jew or Gentile! John chapter 3, verse 16: **"For God so loved the world** [everyone!]**, that he gave his only begotten Son".** This is not rocket science!

Please turn to Psalm 49. Like I say, you cannot save yourself. Your goodness, your self-righteousness, as far as the Lord is concerned, is as filthy rags. Look at verse 6, please. Psalm 49, verse 6: **"They that trust in their wealth, and boast themselves in the multitude of their riches; None** *of them* **can by any means redeem his brother, nor give to God a ransom for him: (For the redemption of their soul** *is* **precious, and it ceaseth for ever)."** You cannot redeem your own soul, in reference here to purgatory. Here, the Scripture's very clear. You cannot redeem your brother's soul, or your soul, or any soul, for that matter, meaning your works cannot save you. It's all of God. One more time: He owns everything. He does not need you to do anything. All He asks is for you to believe on Him. One more time: get on your knees and say, **"God, be merciful to me, a sinner."** And even your wealth cannot save you, found here very clearly in verse 6.

One more Scripture to share with you, before this broadcast ends. Psalm 52. Take a look at verse 7, please: **"Lo, *this is* the man *that* made not God his strength; but trusted in the abundance of his riches, *and* strengthened himself in his wickedness." "It is easier for a camel to go through the eye of a needle, than for a rich man to enter into the kingdom of Heaven"** (Matthew 19:24). One more time, get on your knees and say, **"God, be merciful to me, a sinner!"** Then trust Him, take Him as your own Saviour.

**VERSES 5:7: For Moses describeth the righteousness which is of the law, That the man which doeth those things shall live by them. But the righteousness which is of faith speaketh on this wise, Say not in thine heart, Who shall ascend into heaven? (that is, to bring Christ down *from above*:)Or, Who shall descend into the deep? (that is, to bring up Christ again from the dead.)**

Chapter 4, the apostle Paul quoted David and Abraham, two of the greats from the Old Testament, which very clearly demonstrated in their writings how man has always been saved by faith in the one true God. And here, Paul quotes Moses in verse 5, stating very clearly that those that keep the law have to do everything that is contained in the law. And Galatians tells us that if you don't keep everything, if you don't fulfil everything, and if you don't obey everything in the law, you are cursed.

And verses 6 and 7, in my mind, are almost a rebuke against Roman catholicism, their blasphemous view of transubstantiation — the doctrine where the priest, they believe, calls Christ down from Heaven, and the Scripture says here, **"Say not in thine heart, Who shall ascend into heaven? (that is, to bring Christ down *from* above)."** You cannot bring Christ down from above! The catholic priest cannot bring Christ down from above during the mass! Therefore, transubstantiation has no place in the New Testament. It has no place in the life of a born-again Bible believer.

And verse 7, **"Who shall descend into the deep? (that is, to bring up Christ again from the dead.)"** You cannot bring Him up from the dead. He's resurrected! And you cannot bring Him down from Heaven, because He has ascended! He is now seated at the right hand of God. His work is finished. His sacrifice and atonement has been accomplished! It is finished! John chapter 19, verse 30.

So, clearly, Romans 10, verses 1 down to 7, make it crystal clear how man cannot save himself. Man cannot bribe the Lord. Man is totally lost without God. Trust in the Lord Jesus Christ, and only then will you be saved and pardoned from your sin and go to Heaven when you die. Not Hell, where you deserve, but Heaven.

**VERSES 8-9: "But what saith it? The word is nigh thee, *even* in thy mouth, and in thy heart: that is, the word of faith, which we preach; That if thou shalt confess with thy mouth the Lord Jesus, and shalt believe in thine heart that God hath raised him from the dead, thou shalt be saved."**

Verse 8, the apostle Paul, very carefully and very skilfully, quotes the Old Testament, and he goes on, in verse 9, to quote himself. The Old Testament and the New Testament are joined up by one semi-colon. Why? Because Paul, very carefully and very skilfully, is proving, conclusively, how man has always been saved by faith. Look at verse 8, please, one more time. **"The word is nigh thee** [the Word being the Lord Jesus Christ, and the word being the written word of God], *even* **in thy mouth, and in thy heart: that is, the word of faith, which we preach."** Who else could do this? Who else could so masterfully quote the Old Testament and the New Testament with the subtle difference of just a semi-colon?

And also, please remember and appreciate that the Holy Spirit is the author of the Bible, Old Testament and New Testament. Yes, Moses wrote Deuteronomy, and yes, Paul wrote Romans. But the Holy Spirit is the ultimate Author of the entire Bible, all 66 books. But let's look at verse 9, please, in some more detail: **"that if you"** [singular: not your church, not your father, not your mother, not your priest, not your pastor, not your brother, not your husband, not your son) but "if you shalt confess with your mouth the Lord Jesus [meaning to publicly proclaim your belief in the Lord Jesus Christ], and shalt believe in your heart that God has raised him from the dead, you will be saved." One more time: if you confess with your mouth that Jesus is God [the word "Lord" here is *kurios* in Greek, meaning deity], and if you believe in your heart [a real belief, not a head knowledge but a true belief] that God raised Jesus from the dead, you will be saved. You won't go to Hell when you die, but you will go to Heaven. Once again, the just shall live by faith. Trust in Him! This could not be any clearer.

So, during the last broadcast we looked at verses 8 and 9, and we discovered two things. First of all, how the Old Testament has always been consistent with the New Testament. Even though the Old Testament was written hundreds of years before the New Testament, they are both consistent. Why? Because the Holy Spirit wrote both Testaments. And we also discovered, from verse 9, how a sinner, in order to be saved, must believe that Jesus Christ is God and that God resurrected the Lord Jesus Christ from the dead in order to be saved. God the Father resurrected Him, God the Son resurrected Him, and God the Holy Spirit resurrected Him.

Look at verse 10, please: **"For with the heart man believeth unto righteousness; and with the mouth confession is made unto salvation."**

**"Confess"** in verse 9, and **"confession"** in verse 10. A public confession of faith in the Lord Jesus Christ: Romans chapter 4. And an inward confession of faith in the Lord Jesus Christ: James chapter 2. Again, the Lord looks on the heart. James chapter 2. But man looketh on the outward appearance. Romans chapter 4. The whole Bible fits together nicely, like a jigsaw, if and when you rightly divide the word of truth.

So, at this stage, we are halfway through chapter 10 of the Epistle to the Romans. This could also be called the "Faith Chapter". Paul very carefully and very skilfully outlines how man needs to believe that the Lord Jesus Christ is God and that God raised Him from the dead in order to be saved. In 1 Corinthians chapter 15, Paul also told us that if Christ was not raised from the dead, then we are still in our sins and most miserable people. Therefore, you have to believe in the resurrection of the Lord Jesus Christ in order to be saved, along with His deity. Please don't rob Him of His divinity, of His deity. Jesus Christ is God! Not God the Father, not God the Holy Spirit, but Jesus Christ is God the Son.

So, for today's broadcast, let's start, if we may, in verse 11: **"For the scripture saith, Whosoever believeth on him shall not be ashamed."**

Isaiah 28, in reference to the Lord God of the Bible: Jehovah God, Elohim, El Gibbor, Emmanuel. One more time, the deity, one more time, the divinity the deity of the Lord Jesus Christ is very clearly found here. If you sin against God, only God Himself can forgive you. Therefore, Jesus Christ must be God.

Look at verse 12, please:

**VERSE 12: "For there is no difference between the Jew and the Greek: for the same Lord over all is rich unto all that call upon him."**

All have sinned and come short of the glory of God, and we continue to come short of the glory of God. Jew or Gentile, it makes no difference. We all need a Saviour.

**Chapter 10, verse 13: "For whosoever shall call upon the name of the Lord shall be saved."**

Capital "L", capital "O", capital "R", capital "D" in the Old Testament, always referred to Jehovah God. Go back to the Old Testament, please. Isaiah 28. Joel chapter 2. And you will discover how the apostle Paul is quoting their writings, and they are referring to Jehovah God. And Paul says Jesus is Jehovah God.

**VERSES 14-15: "How then shall they call on him in whom they have not believed? and how shall they believe in him of whom they have not heard? and how shall they hear without a preacher? And how shall they preach, except they be sent? as it is written, How beautiful are the feet of them that preach the gospel of peace, and bring glad tidings of good things!"**

Once again, the apostle Paul links the Old Testament up with the New Testament. But two points, please, from verse 14: **"How then shall they call on him in whom they have not believed? and how shall they believe in him of whom they have not heard?"** Call on Him and believe in Him in order to be saved.

And the latter part of verse 14: **"and how shall they hear without a preacher?"** The last thing the Lord said in Matthew chapter 28 and Mark chapter 16 was to go into all of the world and preach the gospel. The Lord Jesus Christ sent His apostles into the world, and vicariously we have been sent into the world to preach the gospel of the Lord Jesus Christ.

And yet saying that, please let me say this: chapter 1 of the Epistle to the Romans made it very clear how mankind is universally aware of the Lord God of the Bible. He has revelation and he has creation and he has a conscience to prove that God is God. He cannot escape the judgment of God. So even if you lived in a part of the world where the gospel had not been preached, and people had not heard of the Lord Jesus Christ directly, they are still without excuse. Why? Because they have a conscience. They have a creation and they have revelation. So verse 15, as far as I am concerned, is primarily focusing on those that go out with the word of God. Like I say, one more time, chapter 1 tells us that the whole of the world, Jew or Gentile, are totally without excuse. But those that go out with the gospel are here to be praised.

**VERSES 16-21: "But they have not all obeyed the gospel. For Esaias saith, Lord, who hath believed our report? So then faith *cometh* by hearing, and hearing by the word of God. But I say, Have they not heard? Yes verily, their sound went into all the earth, and their words unto the ends of the world. But I say, Did not Israel know? First Moses saith, I will provoke you to jealousy *by them that are* no people, *and* by a foolish nation I will anger you. But Esaias is very bold, and saith, I was found of them that sought me not; I was made manifest unto them that asked not after me. But to Israel he saith, All day long I have stretched forth my hands unto a disobedient and gainsaying people."**

Verse 16, Isaiah, known here as Esaias, is lamenting over the unbelief of the people of Israel. Verse 17, faith comes by hearing and hearing by the word of God. The call goes out to repent, and the more that you hear the word of God, the more you know the word of God, the greater your faith is going to be. Verse 18 follows on from verse 16, where the apostle Paul quotes Psalm 19. Again, only the apostle Paul could so skilfully quote the Old Testament and harmonise it with the New Testament. Psalm 19, the call to repent went to the ends of the world. Here in verse 18, the apostle Paul had taken the gospel to the ends of the world, as had Peter, as had John, as had James.

By verse 19, Moses is now cited, and he told the Jews also in his generation, a stiff-necked and unbelieving people, how the Lord would provoke them to jealousy by a foolish nation, i.e., the Gentiles, i.e., the Church. And finally, in verse 21, the Scripture says, **"All day long I have stretched forth my hands unto a disobedient and gainsaying people",** meaning Israel. The Lord God is not willing that anyone should perish. His love for Israel is unconditional. Yes, here it is in reference primarily to the faithful remnant, the seed that was going to come from Isaac. But here, nevertheless, His love, His focus is on Israel. Not once, not twice, but all day long He's reaching out to Israel. Why? Because He loves them.

# CHAPTER 11

VERSES 1-5: "I say then, Hath God cast away his people? God forbid. For I also am an Israelite, of the seed of Abraham, *of* the tribe of Benjamin. God hath not cast away his people which he foreknew. Wot ye not what the scripture saith of Elias? how he maketh intercession to God against Israel saying, Lord, they have killed thy prophets, and digged down thine altars; and I am left alone, and they seek my life. But what saith the answer of God unto him? I have reserved to myself seven thousand men, who have not bowed the knee to *the image of* Baal. Even so then at this present time also there is a remnant according to the election of grace."

Two points from verses 1 down to 5. Number 1: the apostle Paul is making it very clear how Israel *per se* has not been forsaken. The Lord God has always had a faithful remnant of believing Jews, going back to the time of Abraham unto the end of the Great Tribulation. And number 2: Elias, being Elijah of course, is also cited in reference to not being alone in his own generation. He thought he was the only faithful Jew around in his own generation, a generation of apostasy and a generation of unbelief. And the Scripture says, no, **"I have reserved to myself seven thousand men who have not bowed the knee to *the image of* Baal,"** in reference, one more time, to service, not salvation.

Election, therefore, is never in reference to a person or persons' salvation, but always in reference to a person or persons' service. And these people were foreknown, verse 2, through the Lord's foreknowledge, through the Lord's understanding, and use, I believe, of middle knowledge.

**VERSE 6: "And if by grace, then *is it* no more of works: otherwise grace is no more grace. But if *it be* of works, then it is no more grace: otherwise work is no more work."**

Verse 5, the apostle Paul says even at this present time there is also a remnant of believing Jews according to the election of grace. Peter, Paul, John and Andrew were just a few. There were many Jews (Acts chapter 2) that believed on the Lord Jesus Christ and got saved. And many of them were then chosen, subsequently, for service. It wasn't by their works, verse 6, but by the grace of God.

Everything is down to the grace of God. Even Ephesians chapter 2 tells us, **"For by grace are ye saved through faith; and that not of yourselves."** One more time, it's all about God. Grace, grace, and grace!

So, during the last broadcast we discovered, from verses 1 down to 6, from chapter 11 of the Epistle to the Romans, how the Lord God had chosen and preserved seven thousand men, in the lifetime of the prophet Elijah not to bend the knee to the false image of Baal. These men were already saved, but the Lord preserved them for service, and He revealed it to Elijah to encourage him.

Back in the Book of Genesis there is an account of a pagan king who wanted to sin against God. And the Lord God said, No, I have restrained you, I have stopped you from sinning against me. The Lord God is all-powerful. Clearly!

And so when it comes to the Lord's elect, based on the Lord's election, it is no little thing. He can do whatever He chooses to do. And here He decided to step in and reveal to Elijah how there were seven thousand other men just as faithful as him that had not bowed the knee to the image of Baal. And Elijah was greatly encouraged, as was Paul, found here in verse 5. Even to this present time, there is a faithful remnant, according to the election of grace. Not just the apostles, of course, but many more Bible-believing Jews, around 56 A.D., that had been earmarked for service. Not salvation, one more time, but for service.

**VERSES 7-8: "What then? Israel hath not obtained that which he seeketh for; but the election hath obtained it, and the rest were blinded. (According as it is written, God hath given them the spirit of slumber, eyes that they should not see, and ears that they should not hear;) unto this day."**

To understand verses 7 and 8, we need to go back to the Old Testament. Please turn to the Book of Jeremiah chapter 5 and look at verses 21-22: **"Hear now this, O foolish people, and without understanding; which have eyes, and see not; which have ears, and hear not: Fear ye not me? saith the LORD: will ye not tremble at my presence, which have placed the sand *for* the bound of the sea by a perpetual decree, that it cannot pass it: and though the waves thereof**

**toss themselves, yet can they not prevail; though they roar, yet can they not pass over it?"**

But look at verse 23: **"But these people hath a revolting and a rebellious heart; they are revolted and gone."** In reference to Israel, first of all, in the time of Jeremiah, but ultimately, in the time when the Lord Jesus Christ was going to come. Foretold here in the Book of Jeremiah. They chose to reject the Lord Jesus Christ in time, and so through foreknowledge, the Lord God has now judged them.

So, last time we were reading verses 7 and 8, from Romans chapter 11, and I took you back to Jeremiah to show you how the Old Testament prophet prophesised as to how the children of Israel would respond corporately and universally when the Lord Jesus Christ arrived. Unbelief! Much like the Old Testament people did when their prophets called them to repent. And as a result of unbelieving Israel rejecting the Lord Jesus Christ, He – the Lord God – like He did with Pharaoh, hardened their hearts.

But for the sake of the faithful and believing and still future remnant which were going to believe on the Lord Jesus Christ, we discover the following in Matthew chapter 13, verse 13, Jesus speaking: **"Therefore speak I to them in parables: because they seeing see not; and hearing they hear not, neither do they understand."** The Lord had to speak in parables to the people of Israel, because for the most part, only a tiny minority were ever going to believe on Him, and so for the sake of the elect, the Lord Jesus Christ chose parables. The rest of unbelieving Israel were under the judgment. Jeremiah chapter 5 and also Isaiah chapter 6.

And so God, foreseeing this high treason, through His foreknowledge, inspired King David to write the following.

**VERSES 9-10: "And David saith, Let their table be made a snare, and a trap, and a stumblingblock, and a recompense unto them: Let their eyes be darkened, that they may not see, and bow down their back alway."**

So, here, the Lord God holds them (the unbelieving people of Israel) personally responsible for not believing in the Messiah of Israel. They chose to reject Him based on their own free will. It was not His choice, it was not His will that the people of Israel would universally reject Him. But it was foretold, Isaiah chapter 6 and Jeremiah chapter 5, hundreds of years prior to the birth and death and burial of the Lord Jesus Christ. So, sadly and tragically, these unbelieving Jews died in their sins. Their choice, like I say. Nobody made them reject the Lord Jesus Christ. Nobody made them become unbelieving or doubtful or apostate. And so God, seeing what they would do, commissioned the Old Testament prophets to write what was going to occur when the Lord Jesus Christ came on the earth. One more time, it was their own choice. They decided to reject Him. Not the Lord God, but mankind.

**Chapter 11, verses 11-16: "I say then, Have they stumbled that they should fall? God forbid: but *rather* through their fall salvation *is come* unto the Gentiles, for to provoke them to jealousy. Now if the fall of them *be* the riches of the**

**world, and the diminishing of them the riches of the Gentiles; how much more their fulness? For I speak to you Gentiles, inasmuch as I am the apostle of the Gentiles, I magnify mine office: If by any means I may provoke to emulation *them which are* my flesh, and might save some of them. For if the casting away of them *be* the reconciling of the world, what *shall* the receiving *of them be*, but life from the dead? For if the firstfruit *be* holy, the lump *is* also *holy*: and if the root *be* holy, so *are* the branches."**

Romans 11:11 makes it very clear that the Jews have not permanently stumbled. Temporarily, yes, but permanently, no. And through their fall, we, the believing Church, have temporarily replaced Israel. And now, it is our job to provoke them to jealousy, so they, too, repent and believe on the Lord Jesus Christ in order to be saved.

In verse 14, Paul, as an evangelist, is once again wearing his heart on his sleeve. He wanted his own people to be saved. Chapter 9 and chapter 10: and here he says he hopes to provoke to emulation – an old word for jealousy – **"*them which are* my flesh and might save some of them."** Paul was an evangelist. You should be an evangelist. We are all soul-winners for the Lord Jesus Christ. Our roles, our ministries, may differ, but if we are saved, we too are going to want our friends and our family to be saved as well.

In verse 15, he says, **"if the casting away of them *be* the reconciling of the world, what *shall* the receiving *of them be*, but life from the dead?"**

Not a physical resurrection of course, but a spiritual resurrection. And verse 15 makes it very clear that the Lord God of the Bible has not yet finished with Israel. Once the end of the Church age comes, He (the Lord God) is going to switch His attention back to Israel, the house of Jacob. And for any professing Christian that holds to replacement theology, which is purely anti-Semitic, look at verse 16 carefully: **"For if the firstfruit *be* holy, the lump is also *holy*: and if the root *be* holy, so *are* the branches."** The root being Israel. The root is holy, and we are grafted in to the root.

**VERSES 17-18: "And if some of the branches be broken off, and thou, being a wild olive tree, wert graffed in among them, and with them partakest of the root and fatness of the olive tree; Boast not against the branches. But if thou boast, thou bearest not the root, but the root thee."**

No Jews, no Jesus. Salvation is of the Jews. The root is Israel, and we have temporarily replaced Israel, that much is true. But this is only temporary. A day with the Lord is as a thousand years, meaning time is nothing. Time is irrelevant as far as the Lord God is concerned. Don't boast. Don't sneer. Don't mock the Jews because they are in unbelief. Temporarily, yes, we have replaced them. Temporarily, yes, we are the people of God. But one more time: no Jews, no Jesus. No Jesus, no salvation.

**VERSES 19-21: "Thou wilt say then, The branches were broken off, that I might be graffed in. Well; because of unbelief they were broken off, and thou standest by faith. Be not highminded, but fear: For if God spared not the natural branches, *take heed* lest he also spare not thee."**

It's true: the Lord figuratively cut down the tree! It's true: the Lord figuratively cursed the tree! Two occasions are found in the Gospel of Matthew. Chapter 3, where John the Baptist tells us that **"the axe is laid unto the root of the trees"** (verse 10), and he goes on to tell us how **"every tree which bringeth forth not good fruit is hewn down, and cast into the fire."**

And from Matthew chapter 21, we discover the tree that the Lord Jesus Christ cursed. Look at verse 19, please: **"And when he saw a fig tree in the way, he came to it, and found nothing thereon, but leaves only, and said unto it, Let no fruit grow on thee henceforward for ever. And presently the fig tree withered away."** This tree is a picture of unbelieving and apostate Israel. And here the

Lord Jesus Christ has cursed it. Why? Because it is barren.

Please go back to Romans chapter 11. So, very quickly, just before this broadcast ends. From verses 18 down to 21: the root is Israel and the branches are Israel, but we the Gentiles, we the Church are grafted in. We are the equivalent to a wild olive tree. And so Paul warns us how the Lord God did not hesitate to break off the branches in reference to unbelieving Israel.

And in verse 20 he says, **"thou standest by faith." "The just shall live by faith."** But **"Be not highminded, but fear: For if God** [verse 21] **spared not the natural branches** [Why? Because they would not believe on the Lord Jesus Christ. They wanted to be saved by their faith and works, and that's not how this works], *take heed* **lest he also spare not thee."**

Like the Galatians, like the Corinthians, two different groups of people that were saved but at times wanted to go back to the law. They fell from grace. And Paul says: don't you do that! Paul is warning the Gentiles. Paul is warning the Church. Verse 21, one more time: **"For if God spared not the natural branches** [Israel], ***take heed*** **lest he also spare not thee."** Be careful, my friends. Don't fall from grace!

**VERSE 22: "Behold therefore the goodness and severity of God: on them which fell, severity; but toward thee, goodness, if thou continue in *his* goodness: otherwise thou also shalt be cut off."**

The term *cut off* can mean to put someone to death. Like Ananias and Sapphira, Acts chapter 5. The sin unto death. Just look at the Corinthians, the carnal Christians. They were saved, but they fell from grace. They would not repent, so the Lord cut them off. They did not lose their salvation, but they lost their lives. Also from verse 22, I believe the apostle Paul is making the case one more time how Jesus Christ is the only way to be saved. **"I am the way, the truth and the life"** (John 14:6). There is only one mediator between man and God (1 Timothy 2:5). In John 6:66 (an interesting number), it says many of His disciples walked no more with Him. 1 John chapter 2: they went out from us because they were not of us. Where did they go? Back to the law.

Chapter 7, we've already looked at that, how we are dead to the law. We are dead to sin. We are not under the Old Covenant, but we are in the New Covenant. And also from verse 22, this is not in reference to the unpardonable sin. Are you still in doubt?

Look at verse 23, please: **"And they also, if they abide not still in unbelief, shall be graffed in: for God is able to graff them in again."**

The key word from verse 23 is **"unbelief."** Unbelieving Israel. The worst sin a Jew or a Gentile can commit is the sin of unbelief. So, verse 23, please, one more time: **"And they also** [Israel]**, if they abide not still in unbelief** [when it comes to the Person of the Lord Jesus Christ]**, shall be graffed in:** [the branches were broken, but the Lord can reverse that] **for God is able to graff them in again."** He is all-powerful, He can do whatever He chooses to do. He spoke through a donkey. He made the world in six days. He can graft them back in again, if they believe on the Lord Jesus Christ.

**VERSE 24: "For if thou wert cut out of the olive tree which is wild by nature, and wert graffed contrary to nature into a good olive tree: how much more shall these, which be the natural *branches*, be graffed into their own olive tree?"**

Here, a tree represents Israel. Not many trees (plural) but one singular tree. In thy seed (singular) Isaac shall be blessed (Genesis 21:12). And from Isaac, one more time, comes the Lord Jesus Christ. We also discovered, back in verse 16, how the firstfruit is holy. And if the firstfruit be holy, so is the lump, and if the lump be holy, so is the root. Not roots (plural), but root (singular). So, the tree – representing Israel – is God's exclusive means to reach mankind.

So again, we cannot escape the fact that Israel is blessed, Israel has been preserved and Israel was the source of salvation. Salvation is of the Jews. And if you are a saved person, give thanks to Israel, because the root of your foundation is Jewish. Jesus Christ is the foundation of the Church. We are built on Him. And this tree, one more time, represents Israel, and this tree represents the exclusivity of the Lord Jesus Christ. **"I am the way, the truth and the life: no man cometh unto the Father, but by me"** (John 14:6).

Do you want to be saved? Believe on the Lord Jesus Christ. Get down on your knees and say, **"God, be merciful to me, a sinner."** And He will save you the moment you cry out to Him to be saved.

But the main theme from these verses, from chapter 11 (as far as I am concerned) is how the root, and the branches, and the firstfruit are all Jewish. One more time: no Jews, no Jesus. No Jesus, no salvation. Anti-Semitism, therefore, must be discarded. And above that, the Lord God has not done away with Israel. In reference to the faithful remnant, 144,000 Jews are going to be commissioned to preach the gospel around the world.

So, give thanks to the Lord God of Israel! Through the Jews' fall, through the Jews' unbelief, we the Gentiles, we the believing Church, have now been grafted in. So, for here and now, we represent the true people of God. But at the end of the Church age, once the rapture has been and gone, He, the Lord God, is going to go back to Israel. He is the Lord God of Israel, and His love for them is everlasting, and it is unconditional.

**VERSE 25: "For I would not, brethren, that ye should be ignorant of this mystery, lest ye should be wise in your own conceits; that blindness in part is happened to Israel, until the fulness of the Gentiles be come in."**

In reference, I believe, to the end of the Church age. Don't be wise in your own conceits.

Verse 20: Don't be high-minded. Don't be prideful, but fear. **"The fear of the Lord *is* the beginning of wisdom"** (Proverbs 9:10). You stand by faith. Verse 20 as well. **"The just shall live by faith."** You got saved by believing on the Lord Jesus Christ. And you were able to do that because the Jews fell temporarily through unbelief. Verse 25: This is a mystery, something which was not revealed until Paul was called to serve the Lord Jesus Christ. Acts chapter 9, Paul was not chosen to serve the Lord God of the Bible before the foundation of the world, but he was chosen to serve the Lord God once he believed on the Lord Jesus Christ. Also from verse 25 he says how blindness in part has happened to Israel. Not a physical blindness, of course, but a spiritual blindness. And he says it's only happened in part. There were many Bible-believing Jews that did believe on the Lord Jesus Christ, and even to this day there are many more Bible-believing Jews all over the world that believe in the Lord Jesus Christ.

But for me, the main theme from verses 20 down to 25 would be as follows: Jesus Christ is the only sacrifice that God is going to accept. He was the perfect Lamb of God, totally without sin. And by His precious blood, we are saved. But the problem was that many of the Jews went back to the law. They forsook the simplicity which is found in Jesus Christ. And as a result of this, the Lord God cut them off. Again, there is no other way to be saved!

Please turn to 2 Corinthians chapter 11. Look at verse 1, please: **"Would to God ye could bear with me a little in *my* folly: and indeed bear with me. For I am jealous over you with godly jealousy: for I have espoused you to one husband, that I may present *you* as a chaste virgin to Christ. But I fear, lest by any means, as the serpent beguiled Eve through his subtilty, so your minds should be corrupted from the simplicity that is in Christ."** And so, here we discover, by these three simple verses, not to fall into unbelief.

Don't allow the devil to rob you of the simplicity that is found in the Lord Jesus Christ. It happened in John chapter 6: many of His disciples walked no more with Him. In Romans chapter 11, the apostle Paul says: be careful, many of the Jews fell and the Lord subsequently cut them off. Be careful, therefore, that it doesn't happen to you.

**VERSE 26-27: "And so all Israel shall be saved: as it is written, There shall come out of Sion the Deliverer, and shall turn away ungodliness from Jacob: For this *is* my covenant unto them, when I shall take away their sins."**

Not all of Israel without exception are going to be saved, but all of Israel that believes on the Lord Jesus Christ. Here, this is in reference to the believing remnant, those that the Lord is going to preserve, through foreknowledge and through middle knowledge. And among this group of saved and sealed Jews would most certainly be the 144,000 male Jewish evangelists, chosen and preserved and sealed for service during the Great Tribulation.

Also from verses 26 and 27, this is what we call a "split prophecy." The Old Testament prophets wrote about the First Coming of the Lord Jesus Christ and also the Second Coming of the Lord Jesus Christ. Many Jews got saved at His First Coming, but many more are going to be saved at His Second Coming.

So if there was still any doubt as to whom the apostle Paul is speaking about, look at verse 26 and 27, please, one more time: **"There shall come out of Sion** [Israel] **the Deliverer** [the Lord Jesus Christ], **and shall turn away ungodliness from Jacob** [being Israel, of course!]" Verse 27 again: **"For this *is* my covenant unto them** [the Jews], **when I shall take away their sins** [in reference to Israel, of course!]."

He came the first time, Acts chapter 7. He was standing and ready to come back to Israel. But the Jews corporately rejected Him, so the gospel went to the Gentiles. And now He is ready to come back again, but He won't come back until the end of the Church age. He won't come back until the end of the Great Tribulation.

But one more time, He is going to return to Jacob. He is going to return to Israel, and every Jew that believes on Him (verse 26) is going to be saved. Many Jews are going to be saved during the Great Tribulation, in fact, many more than got saved in Acts chapter 2 on the day of Pentecost.

**VERSE 28:** "As concerning the gospel, *they are* enemies for your sakes: but as touching the election, *they are* beloved for the fathers' sakes."

Yes, the Jews crucified and rejected the Lord Jesus Christ. Yes, the Jews rejected many of their prophets and Old Testament kings, and they even rejected God. They wanted Saul to reign over them. It broke the Lord's heart. And yes, there's even a synagogue of Satan to this present day.

And yet we, as Bible-believing Christians, have to love the Jews nevertheless. Why? Because they are loved for their fathers' sakes. For the sake of Abraham, for the sake of Isaac, for the sake of Jacob. The Lord loves Israel.

Yes, they rejected most of their Old Testament prophets and kings. Yes, they rejected the Lord Jesus Christ. And yes, they are enemies for the sake of the gospel, because they do it in ignorance, some wilfully, some not. But nevertheless we have to love them for the sake of their forefathers.

**VERSES 29-32:** "For the gifts and calling of God *are* without repentance. For as ye in times past have not believed God, yet have now obtained mercy through their unbelief: Even so have these also now not believed, that through your mercy they also may obtain mercy. For God hath concluded them all in unbelief, that he might have mercy upon all."

Chapter 9 verse 15, the Scripture saith: **"I will have mercy on whom I will have mercy, and I will have compassion on whom I will have compassion."** Two chapters later, Scripture with Scripture, **"For God hath concluded them all in unbelief, that He might have mercy upon all."** Why? Because of verse 29: **"For the gifts and calling of God *are* without repentance."**

His love for Israel (one more time) is eternal, and it is unconditional. And verses 30 and 31, count your blessings! Because of their unbelief, we the Gentiles, we the Church, were grafted in, that we may provoke them to jealousy. They lost the mercy of God through their own free will as a result of their unbelief. But we, the Gentiles, we the Church, have received the mercy of God. Praise be to God and one more time, count your blessings and thank God that He has saved you.

So, we have very nearly finished Romans chapter 11. Let's call this chapter "the chapter of second chances." The Lord God showed His love to Israel, and He also showed His love to the Church. If you are not saved, you can be saved. **"The just shall live by faith."** If you're not saved, just humble yourself, and say, **"God, please be merciful to me, a sinner."** And if you call on His name, He will save you the moment you call on His name. The Lord's longsuffering and love for Israel was magnificent. And one more time, through their fall, through their period of unbelief, we the Gentiles, we the believing Church, have now been grafted in. Pride and the problem of self-righteousness should not be something that we should ever be guilty of. The Jews tried to save themselves through their faith and works, but we are saved by faith alone.

**VERSE 33-36: "O the depth of the riches both of the wisdom and knowledge of God! how unsearchable *are* his**

**judgments, and his ways past finding out! For who hath known the mind of the Lord? or who hath been his counsellor? Or who hath first given to him, and it shall be recompensed unto him again? For of him, and through him, and to him, *are* all things: to whom *be* glory for ever. Amen."**

Verse 34 is clearly a rhetorical question. Who has known the mind of the Lord? No one. Who hath been his counsellor? No one. Verse 33 almost sounds like Deuteronomy 29:29: **"The secret *things belong* unto the LORD our God."** You will never truly understand who the Lord God of the Bible is, but you must believe on Him. You must trust in Him to do what He said He would do.

And verse 36 is worthy to be read one more time: **"For of him, and through him, and to him, *are* all things: to whom *be* glory for ever. Amen"**, in reference to the Lord God's deity. He is omnipresent, He is omniscient, and He is omnipotent. He is all-powerful. He is all knowing. He is everywhere at the same time, and He knows the thoughts of mankind. So, come to Him, and trust in Him and He will save you to the uttermost. For He is worthy to be worshipped.

# CHAPTER 12

VERSES 1-2: "I beseech you therefore, brethren, by the mercies of God, that ye present your bodies a living sacrifice, holy, acceptable unto God, *which is* your reasonable service. And be not conformed to this world: but be ye transformed by the renewing of your mind, that ye may prove what *is* that good, and acceptable, and perfect, will of God."

In verse 1, Paul says, **"I beseech you therefore, brethren** [I beg you, brothers and sisters] **by the mercies of God, that ye** [all] **present your bodies a living sacrifice." "Be holy for I am holy"** (1 Peter 1:16). Without holiness, no man shall see God (Heb. 12:14).

And in the latter part of verse 1, he says, **"*which is* your reasonable service,"** meaning you are expected to do this. This is the least you should do. Why? Because God is holy. And if He has saved you, He expects you to live holy. He expects you to set a good example. Why? Because the mercy of God was withdrawn temporarily from the Jews. But we the Gentiles were grafted in through their unbelief.

And the Scripture goes on to tell us how we must continue in His goodness, in His holiness. Otherwise we, too, will be cut off. We won't lose our salvation, but we may lose our lives. And I showed you from a previous broadcast how Ananias and

Sapphira were cut off. They lost their lives, but they did not lose their salvation.

But back to verse 1: how are we expected to continue to present our bodies as a living sacrifice? This is something that we are supposed to do every single day of the week. Please turn to Matthew chapter 5. The Roman Catholics believe that if you beat your body, if you whip your body, and if you starve your body, you can beat your body to submission, that somehow you can keep lust at bay. But lust, but sin, comes from within, not without.

Look at Matthew chapter 5 verse 27: **"Ye have heard that it was said by them of old time, Thou shalt not commit adultery: But I say unto you, That whosoever looketh on a woman to lust after her hath committed adultery with her already in his heart. And if thy right eye offend thee, pluck it out, and cast *it* from thee: for it is profitable for thee that one of thy members should perish, and not *that* thy whole body should be cast into hell. And if thy right hand offend thee, cut it off, and cast *it* from thee: for it is profitable for thee that one of thy members should perish, and not *that* thy whole body should be cast into hell."**

Here, the Lord Jesus Christ is describing sin. He's not telling us to physically self-mutilate our hands or our eyes. Why? Because one more time, lust comes from within, not without. This is called letterism when you take every verse of the Bible to be literal. And like I say, the Catholic Church, especially Opus Dei, believe that if they beat themselves, if they whip themselves, and if they starve themselves, they can deal with the problem of sin, they can deal with the problem of lust. And that's not how you should do this.

Please go back to Romans chapter 12. So the best way to harmonise Matthew chapter 5 and Romans chapter 12 is to look in more detail at verse 2: **"And be not conformed to this world: but be ye transformed by the renewing of your mind, that ye may prove what *is* that good, and acceptable, and perfect, will of God."**

How can you do that? By reading the word of God. How will you ever know the will of God if you don't know the word of God? You should meditate on the Scriptures every single day. So that is how you get control over your flesh and that is how you gain victory over sin. And that is what Paul means when he says to present your bodies as a living sacrifice unto God. Meditate, meditate and meditate!

So, during the last broadcast we looked at the problem of sin and of lust. And I showed you from Matthew chapter 5 how severe the Lord Jesus Christ took sin. And He said: pluck your eyes out and cut your hands off. But not literally, of course. In a spiritual and a figurative sense!

So, I took you back to Romans chapter 12 to ascertain how we are supposed to get victory over sin, how we are supposed to get victory over lust, or sin in general. It makes no difference. And Paul told us to renew our minds daily by the reading of the word of God, to read the Scriptures every single day. Meditate, meditate and meditate. Don't suppress sin. Don't suppress your feelings, but bring them to the Lord Jesus Christ!

Submit yourself to Him and then go back to the word of God. Read the Scriptures. That's the only way you'll ever get peace and power in your life.

But for today's broadcast, let's start, if we may, in verse 3: **"For I say, through the grace given unto me, to every man that is among you, not to think** *of himself* **more highly than he ought to think; but to think soberly, according as God hath dealt to every man the measure of faith."**

Humble yourself and annihilate the problem of pride. Chapter 11, verse 20: **"Be not highminded but fear"**. **"The fear of the LORD** *is* **the beginning of wisdom"** (Proverbs 9:10).

James chapter 4, verse 6: **"God resisteth the proud, but giveth grace unto the humble."** The devil fell through the sin of pride. Be careful you don't fall through the sin of pride.

And finally the latter part of Romans chapter 12, verse 3: **"but to think soberly, according as God hath dealt to every man the measure of faith."** There are different types of faith, and there are different types of callings and ministries. Some people are called to be evangelists, some people are called to be Bible teachers, and some people are called to be street preachers. Many callings, but not the same ministry.

So, last time we ended in verse 3 from Romans chapter 12, where the apostle Paul told us **"according as God hath dealt to every man the measure of faith."** While it's true we are all called and we are all saved the same way, it's rare for two people to then be given the same ministry. Salvation, therefore, is one thing, whereas service is something else altogether.

Look at verses 4-8, please: **"For as we have many members in one body, and all members have not the same office: So we, *being* many, are one body in Christ, and every one members one of another. Having then gifts differing according to the grace that is given to us, whether prophecy, *let us prophesy* according to the proportion of faith; Or ministry, *let us wait* on *our* ministering: or he that teacheth, on teaching; Or he that exhorteth, on exhortation: he that giveth, *let him do it* with simplicity; he that ruleth, with diligence; he that sheweth mercy, with cheerfulness."**

So, verses 4 down to 8 make it very clear how the Lord God of the Bible equips saved people in different ways. Salvation is one thing, service is something else. No two people will have the same calling or ministry. It's very rare, like I say, for two people to have the same calling. But verses 4 down to 8 make it very clear how we all have at least one gift when it comes to serving the Lord.

**VERSES 9-14: "*Let* love be without dissimulation. Abhor that which is evil; cleave to that which is good. Be kindly affectioned one to another with brotherly love; in honour preferring one another; Not slothful in business; fervent in spirit; serving the Lord; Rejoicing in hope; patient in tribulation; continuing instant in prayer; Distributing to the necessity of saints; given to hospitality. Bless them which persecute you: bless, and curse not."**

Verses 9 down to 14 almost appear, they almost sound, they almost feel like the words from the Lord Jesus Christ during his famous "Sermon on the Mount" sermon. And of course, the

Sermon on the Mount is primarily for the Jews under the law. But here, Paul is speaking to us – the Gentiles – in the Church age. Scripture with Scripture, and you can easily harmonise parts of the New Testament. The law and grace. The gospels and the epistles.

Matthew chapter 5, look at verse 11, please. **"Blessed are ye, when *men* shall revile you, and persecute *you*, and shall say all manner of evil against you falsely, for my sake."**

Back to Romans chapter 12. Look at verse 12 again, please: **"Rejoicing in hope; patient in tribulation; continuing instant in prayer."** Rejoice in the Lord always. Verse 13: **"Distributing to the necessity of saints; given to hospitality."** If you can help and support someone who is in need, you should do so! **"Faith without works is dead"** (James 2:26).

**VERSES 15-21:** **"Rejoice with them that do rejoice, and weep with them that weep. *Be* of the same mind one toward another. Mind not high things, but condescend to men of low estate. Be not wise in your own conceits. Recompense to no man evil for evil. Provide things honest in the sight of all men. If it be possible, as much as lieth in you, live peaceably with all men. Dearly beloved, avenge not yourselves, but *rather* give place unto wrath: for it is written, Vengeance *is* mine; I will repay, saith the Lord. Therefore if thine enemy hunger, feed him; if he thirst, give him drink: for in so doing thou shalt heap coals of fire on his head. Be not overcome of evil, but overcome evil with good."**

Turn the other cheek. One more time, Paul here is very much in harmony with the Sermon on the Mount. Verse 19: **"for it is written, Vengeance *is* mine; I will repay, saith the Lord."** It's not easy to turn the other cheek. It's not easy to forgive someone who has wronged you. But, you must do so! The Lord is going to pour out His fury on His enemies at the time of His choosing.

Verse 15: **"Rejoice with them that do rejoice, and weep with them that weep."** Laugh with the world, and the world laugh with you; cry, and you cry alone. But here Paul makes it very clear how we, the Church, should rejoice together, and how we, as the Church, should weep together as well.

Verse 16: Humble yourselves again. Annihilate pride. Condescend to men of low estate. Never mind those at the top or the well-to-do people, condescend to men of low estate. Get down on your knees and humble yourself! Verse 18: be a good neighbour if you can. Verse 20: if your enemy is hungry, feed him; if he is thirsty, give him a drink! Matthew chapter 25 also echoes what the apostle Paul is telling us here.

And verse 21, one more time: **"Be not overcome of evil, but overcome evil with good."** Turn the other cheek. Rise above it. Let your testimony shine to the world.

And finally, and just before we conclude chapter 12, from verse 9, I forgot to look at it during the last broadcast, and the apostle Paul tells us: **"*Let* love be without dissimulation. Abhor that which is evil; cleave to that which is good."** Stand up for that which is good and defend godliness, and at the same time, shun sin and expose everything that is evil.

# CHAPTER 13

V ERSE 1: "Let every soul be subject unto the higher powers. For there is no power but of God: the powers that be are ordained of God."

Whether you are saved or not, the Lord God of the Bible expects everyone to submit to the powers that be. Governments are ordained by the Lord God of the Bible.

Please turn to John chapter 19. Look at verse 10, please: **"Then saith Pilate unto him, Speakest thou not unto me? knowest thou not that I have power to crucify thee, and have power to release thee? Jesus answered, Thou couldest have no power *at all* against me, except it were given thee from above: therefore he that delivered me unto thee hath the greater sin."**

Please turn to Daniel chapter 2. Look at verse 19: **"Then was the secret revealed unto Daniel in a night vision. Then Daniel blessed the God of Heaven. Daniel answered and said, Blessed be the name of God for ever and ever: for wisdom and might are his: And he changeth the times and the seasons: he removeth kings, and setteth up kings: he giveth wisdom unto the wise, and knowledge to them that know understanding: He revealeth the deep and secret things: he knoweth what *is* in the darkness, and the light dwelleth with him."**

Please turn back to Romans chapter 13. Verse 1, one more time: **"Let every soul be subject unto the higher powers. For there is no power but of God: the powers that be are ordained of God."** John chapter 19, we read where the Lord Jesus Christ is standing in the presence of Pilate, the governor of Israel. And He says to Pilate: you could have no authority unless it was given to you from above.

The Lord God of the Bible is totally sovereign. In Daniel chapter 2, He says the same thing, how the Lord God changes the times and the seasons, and He even removes kings and sets up kings. The Lord God can do whatever He chooses to do.

So, make sure you are not an anarchist. As a child is in submission to its parents, and their parents are in submission to their employers, so you must be in submission to the State. But I will say this, very briefly: when the State tells you to do something that the word of God tells you not to do, you follow the word of God. You follow your conscience.

During the last broadcast we were looking at how the Lord God of the Bible has ordained the powers that be. All of the world governments are under His control. They may not all be saved governments. You may have unsaved politicians all over the world. But, nevertheless, they are there by the decree of the Lord God of the Bible. And I told you how the Scripture makes it very clear how we are to obey those that are in authority.

Please turn to Acts chapter 5. Let's start, if we may, in verse 26: **"Then went the captain with the officers, and brought them without violence: for they feared the people, lest they** should have been stoned. And when they had brought them, they set *them* before the council: and the high priest asked them, Saying, Did not we straitly command you that ye should not teach in this name? and, behold, ye have filled Jerusalem with your doctrine, and intend to bring this man's blood upon us. Then Peter and the *other* apostles answered and said, We ought to obey God rather than men."

Please turn to Matthew chapter 12. Look at verse 18: **"Behold my servant, whom I have chosen; my beloved, in whom my soul is well pleased: I will put my spirit upon him, and he shall shew judgment to the Gentiles. He shall not strive, nor cry; neither shall any man hear his voice in the streets."** He won't be an anarchist, He won't be somebody who is known to cause civil disobedience. The Lord Jesus Christ came to die for the sins of the world. He did not come to cause a revolution. He did not come to overthrow world governments. He did not come to abolish capitalism.

Please go back to Romans chapter 13. So one more time: submit yourselves to the government. Acts chapter 5 made it very clear how when the words of men supersede the words of God, you go with the word of God. Men come and go, but the Lord God does not change. **"I am the LORD, I change not."** (Malachi 3:6)

**VERSE 2: "Whosoever therefore resisteth the power, resisteth the ordinance of God: and they that resist shall receive to themselves damnation".**

Meaning judgment! If you don't submit to the authority, you are going to be punished. Pure and simple! If you break the law, for example, they will arrest you and put you into jail. They have the right and the authority, from Heaven, believe it or not, to do that!

**VERSE 3-4: "For rulers are not a terror to good works, but to the evil. Wilt thou then not be afraid of the power? do that which is good, and thou shalt have praise of the same: For he is the minister of God to thee for good. But if thou do that which is evil, be afraid; for he beareth not the sword in vain: for he is the minister of God, a revenger to *execute* wrath upon him that doeth evil."**

Verse 3: Rulers – governments, those in authority – are not there to cause terror to those that do good works, but they are there to punish evildoers. And Paul says if you don't want to be afraid of the power of the governments, do that which is good, and when you do that which is good, they will praise you! And verse 4 is fascinating: **"For he is the minister of God to thee for good."**

It could be your prime minister, it could be your president, it could be your king or it could be your queen. It makes no difference. They are ministers of God, ordained by God. And he goes on to say: "But if thou do that which is evil, be afraid; [why?] for he beareth not the sword in vain: for he [president, king, prime minister or queen] is the minister [servant] of God, a revenger to *execute* wrath upon him that doeth evil."

So, it really is crystal clear. The powers that be are ordained of God. They have a right to do what they do. It may be you live in a far-away country where the leaders of your nation don't even believe in the Lord God of the Bible. It makes no difference. They are there solely at His decree. Look at 1 Peter, please. Chapter 2, verse 17: **"Honour all *men*. Love the brotherhood. Fear God. Honour the king."** Take a look at 1 Timothy, chapter 2, verse 1: **"I exhort therefore, that, first of all, supplications, prayers, intercessions, *and* giving of thanks, be made for all men; For kings, and *for* all that are in authority; that we may lead a quiet and peaceable life in all godliness and honesty."**

So, the entire Bible is so very clear: submit to the authority and pray for those that are in authority. It makes no difference, like I said, if they believe on the Lord Jesus Christ or not. It makes no difference if they are a godly government or a godless government. You are to pray for them because God has ordained them to be His ministers.

**VERSE 5-7:** **"Wherefore *ye* must needs be subject, not only for wrath, but also for conscience sake. For for this cause pay ye tribute also: for they are God's ministers, attending continually upon this very thing. Render therefore to all their dues: tribute to whom tribute *is due*; custom to whom custom; fear to whom fear; honour to whom honour."**

Verse 6 is elementary: no taxes, no State. The Lord God of the Bible is a God of order, not confusion. The Bible, therefore, is a book of common sense. But you need to use your common sense when you read the word of God.

Verse 5: You must be in submission to the State, not only for your conscience's sake, but also for wrath. Because if you break the law, you will be prosecuted and in some cases, verse 4, you could even be put to death!

And finally, from verse 7: **"tribute to whom tribute *is due*; custom to whom custom; fear to whom fear; honour to whom honour."** Paul, when he met those in authority, was very respectful. He was also very polite and very courteous. Yes, he called sin, sin; and he also preached holiness and righteousness when he was able to, but above all, he appreciated that the powers to be were ordained by the Lord God of the Bible.

**VERSE 8: "Owe no man any thing; but to love one another: for he that loveth another hath fulfilled the law."**

This love comes once you are born again. Before you were born again, you were dead in your trespasses and sins, but the moment the Lord regenerates you, He gives you a new heart and now you can love the brethren and you can also love the lost. So the moment you love mankind, you have (past tense) fulfilled the law. And remember, we are not under the law. We are not under the Old Covenant. We are under the grace of God. We are in Christ Jesus. We are very much part of the New Covenant.

**VERSE 9: "For this, Thou shalt not commit adultery, Thou shalt not kill, Thou shalt not steal, Thou shalt not bear false witness, Thou shalt not covet; and if *there be* any other commandment, it is briefly comprehended in this saying, namely, Thou shalt love thy neighbour as thyself."**

Please appreciate that verses 8 and 9 are addressed to saved people. Nothing from verses 8 and 9 could save you. This is what happens once you are saved, once you have been regenerated. And like I say, from verse 8, this love is for the brethren. Verse 9, this love is for the world. For God so loved the world! If He loves the world, we should love the world as well. But we don't associate with the world. We are in the world, but we are not part of the world's system. Be in the world, but not of the world.

And yet, saying that, please allow me to say this: while it's true that the Lord has a love for the world, His ultimate love is for the Church. So, we have a love for the world, but our ultimate love is for Him. So, please be wise and careful when it comes to appreciating God's love for the world and His love for the Church. Our love for the world and our love for the Lord.

And finally, for this broadcast, please look at verse 10: **"Love worketh no ill to his neighbour: therefore love *is* the fulfilling of the law."**

This is self-sacrifice and self-denial on the part of a saved person in the attempt to try and reach out through the power of the Holy Spirit to try and reach into the life, into the heart of an unsaved person and reach out to them and present the gospel of the Lord Jesus Christ to them. We can do it because the triune God lives within us. And once you have done it (verse 10), you have (past tense) fulfilled the law.

**Chapter 13, verse 11-14: "And that, knowing the time, that now *it is* high time to awake out of sleep: for now *is* our**

**salvation nearer than when we believed. The night is far spent, the day is at hand: let us therefore cast off the works of darkness, and let us put on the armour of light. Let us walk honestly, as in the day; not in rioting and drunkenness, not in chambering and wantonness, not in strife and envying. But put ye on the Lord Jesus Christ, and make not provision for the flesh, to *fulfil* the lusts *thereof*."**

Verse 11: **"awake out of your sleep,"** meaning, if you are apathetic, if you have backslidden, repent! Turn from it and come back to the Lord. Why? Because our salvation is nearer than when we first believed, meaning the rapture could be imminent. Verse 12: **"The night is far spent, the day is at hand"**. The rapture could come at a moment's notice. And he goes on to say "let us therefore cast off the works of darkness."

One more time: if you are apathetic, if you have backslidden, turn from it! **"Be ye holy; for I am holy"** (1 Peter 1:16). Without holiness, no man shall see the Lord. (Heb. 12:14).

And he goes on to say "put on the armour of light", being the Lord Jesus Christ, of course, in verse 14. But verse 13 he says, "Let us walk honestly, as in the day; not in rioting and drunkenness." Why? Because the world is watching you! You have to love your neighbour. We saw that in verse 9 and verse 10.

You need to have a clean testimony. Your life should reflect the goodness and glory, and sinlessness even, of the Lord Jesus Christ. You won't be sinless yourself, of course not. But, your life should be cleaner, your life should be much better than unsaved people.

And finally, two points in reference to verse 14: **"put ye on the Lord Jesus Christ."** All of you, put on the Lord Jesus Christ, meaning walk in the Spirit. Don't go back to the Old Testament. Don't go back to the law. Don't try to better yourself in your own physical way. Everything that you do should be done through the Holy Spirit and through the power of the Lord Jesus Christ.

And the second point from verse 14, **"make not provision for the flesh, to *fulfil* the lusts thereof."** Why? Because God is holy! Again, the world is watching you, and He, God, wants you to arrive at the Judgment Seat of Christ and receive a full reward. You won't do that, my friends, if you are sinful, if you are carnal. But if you repent, if you turn from your backslidden ways, if you awake out of your apathy, if you confess your sins to Him, He, God, is faithful and just to cleanse you of all of your unrighteousness, and to restore you unto full fellowship with Him.

# CHAPTER 14

VERSE 1-3: "Him that is weak in the faith receive ye, *but* not to doubtful disputations. For one believeth that he may eat all things: another, who is weak, eateth herbs. Let not him that eateth despise him that eateth not; and let not him which eateth not judge him that eateth: for God hath received him."

Verses 1 to 3 are not speaking about a person's physical weakness, but their spiritual weakness. Verse 1: he that is weak in the faith receive him. Verse 2: for one believes he can eat anything, another, who is weak, eateth herbs, meaning some of these early Christians had very sensitive consciences. Why? Because many of them, before they got saved, were sacrificing food to animals! They thought certain types of food were sacred, and once they got saved they were still battling some of their old natures, and Paul says in verse 3: **"Let not him that eateth despise him that eateth not; and let not him which eateth not judge him that eateth: [why?] for God hath received him."** The just shall live by faith! You got saved by believing on the Lord Jesus Christ. You did not get saved by being a vegetarian or a meat-eater.

Please turn to 1 Corinthians chapter 8. Take a look at verse 8, please: **"But meat commendeth us not to God: for neither, if we eat, are we the better; neither, if we eat not, are we the worse."** The Lord God couldn't care less what you eat.

All dietary laws and restrictions have been done away with in Christ Jesus. And please allow me to show you one more Scripture, if I may. 1 Corinthians chapter 7, take a look at verse 24, please: **"Brethren, let every man, wherein he is called, therein abide with God."**

So, if you were a meat-eater when the Lord God called you to salvation, remain a meat-eater. If you were a vegetarian when the Lord God called you to salvation, remain a vegetarian. It makes no difference to the Lord. We are all under grace. We can do whatever we wish to do. Within reason, of course. But when it comes to food, all food is pure.

So, please turn back to Romans chapter 14. Rest in the Lord Jesus Christ. Enjoy your liberty in the Lord Jesus Christ. But don't cause your brethren to stumble. More on that in the next broadcast.

So, during the last broadcast, we saw very clearly how the Christian has great liberty in the Lord Jesus Christ. If you were called as a meat-eater, remain as you are. If you were called as a vegetarian, remain as you are. But if you are weak in the faith, pray to the Lord for wisdom, and He will give it to you, but above all, you have to help yourself. You must be reading the word of God each and every day.

So for today's broadcast, if we may, let's begin in verse 4: **"Who art thou that judgest another man's servant? to his own master he standeth or falleth. Yea, he shall be holden up: for God is able to make him stand."**

So, stop interfering in the life of other Christians! The Judaizers were very good at going around and trying to get people to go back to the law, to restrict themselves on what they could or could not eat. They did it to Paul on many occasions, but we are under grace, not under the law. And take a look at the latter part of verse 4: **"for God is able to make him stand."**

He has already saved us to the uttermost. We came to Him in our worst possible states, and He has received us and He has forgiven us. Like I said last time: it makes no difference whether you are a meat-eater or a vegetarian.

Have you repented, have you believed on the Lord Jesus Christ? That's what saves you, not what you eat, or don't eat, for that matter. And I will say this also, if I may, as a word of warning: don't cause those that are weak in the faith to stumble, because if you do, the Lord God is going to punish you.

Take a look, please, at Matthew chapter 18. Let's start, if we may, in verse 4: **"Whosoever therefore shall humble himself as this little child, the same is greatest in the kingdom of heaven."** Jump down to verse 6: **"But whoso shall offend one of these little ones which believe in me, it were better for him that a millstone were hanged about his neck, and *that* he were drowned in the depth of the sea. Woe unto the world because of offences! for it must needs be that offences come; but woe to that man by whom the offence cometh!"**

So, be warned and be careful how you treat someone who is weak in the faith. If you cause someone to stumble, who is weak in the faith, the Lord Jesus Christ is going to punish you. So, be very careful and mindful not to invade their liberty and as a result of that, push them back under the law. The law cannot save them, the law will condemn them. Be very careful indeed!

**VERSES 5-6: "One man esteemeth one day above another: another esteemeth every day *alike*. Let every man be fully persuaded in his own mind. He that regardeth the day, regardeth *it* unto the Lord; and he that regardeth not the day, to the Lord he doth not regard *it*. He that eateth, eateth to the Lord, for he giveth God thanks; and he that eateth not, to the Lord he eateth not, and giveth God thanks."**

Verses 5 and 6 continue on from verses 1 down to 4, in reference to one's liberty in the Lord Jesus Christ. You can do whatever you choose to do, within reason, of course. You can eat (and we looked at this in the last broadcast) whatever you choose to eat. And you can worship the Lord on whatever day you choose to worship Him on. Why? Because you have great liberty in the Lord Jesus Christ. Some Christians meet on a Monday, some Christians meet on a Tuesday, some Christians meet on a Wednesday, some Christians meet on a Thursday, some Christians meet on a Friday, and some Christians even meet on a Saturday, to keep the Jewish Sabbath. You can do whatever you choose to do. Just don't teach it as doctrine. Just don't attack those that don't do what you wish to do.

And also from verses 5 and 6 comes the subject of Christmas and Easter. Can I celebrate Christmas? Can I celebrate Easter?

You have great liberty in the Lord Jesus Christ, one more time, to do whatever you choose to do. Just don't condemn those that don't agree with you and don't force those to conform to your way of worship. One more time, from verse 5: **"Let every man be fully persuaded in his own mind."**

**VERSES 7-8: "For none of us liveth to himself, and no man dieth to himself. For whether we live, we live unto the Lord; and whether we die, we die unto the Lord: whether we live therefore, or die, we are the Lord's."**

It's all about God. Don't use your liberty to cause someone to sin. Rejoice in the Lord God. Rest in Him. But above all, don't allow yourself, don't allow your liberty to cause someone else to stumble, to fall and to be offended. Because if you do, one more time, the Lord God is going to chastise you and He is going to punish you until you repent and come back to the simplicity that is in Christ Jesus.

**VERSE 9: "For to this end Christ both died, and rose, and revived, that he might be Lord both of the dead and living."**

The latter part of verse 9 says how He, Christ, might be Lord both of the dead and living. Quite simply, those that died believing on the Lord Jesus Christ and are now with Him are in submission to Him. He is their Lord and they are in Heaven with Him now worshipping Him, and the living would be those of us alive today that are awaiting His return for us in the air! The rapture, of course!

**VERSE 10: "But why dost thou judge thy brother? or why dost thou set at nought thy brother? for we shall all stand before the judgment seat of Christ."**

We the Church are going to be judged at the Judgment Seat of Christ, the Bema Seat. The Great White Throne Judgment is reserved for unsaved people, but we the Church are going to be judged. Not in reference to our salvation, but more in reference to the crowns that we are going to receive once we enter unto the presence of the Lord Jesus Christ. And of course, many of us will have to stand in the presence of the Lord Jesus Christ and give an account of how we lived after we had been saved, more in reference to our service, not our salvation. Thank God we are not going to be judged like the world will be judged at the Great White Throne Judgment.

But here, Paul is once again pushing the point home: stop judging your brother; he will be judged just as you will be judged, at the Judgment Seat of Christ. So, please, the apostle Paul is saying: stop judging one another and rejoice in the finished work of the Lord Jesus Christ.

So during the last broadcast we discovered how we the Church are going to have to appear at the Judgment Seat of the Lord Jesus Christ, not in reference to our salvation, but in reference to our service and also in reference to how we treated one another. So, don't fret and don't worry, when it comes to how person A, B or C lives and operates. It's not your concern. If they fall into sin, that's one thing, but what they do when it comes to what they eat or which day they choose to worship the Lord God of the Bible, it is not of your concern.

**VERSES 11-12: "For it is written, *As* I live, saith the Lord, every knee shall bow to me, and every tongue shall confess to God. So then every one of us shall give account of himself to God."**

Verse 11, **"*As* I live, saith the Lord, every knee shall bow to me, and every tongue shall confess to God."** Whether you are saved or not, you will bend the knee and you will confess that Jesus Christ is God. But here explicitly, Paul is referring to the state of the born-again Bible believer when he comes into the presence of Almighty God. He/she will bend the knee. He/she shall confess to the Lord. He knows everything anyway.

But go back to the Book of Genesis, and there you discover the Lord God of the Bible calling out to Adam: where art thou, Adam? He knew where Adam was, but He wanted Adam to come forth and confess to Him. And here, the apostle Paul is saying the same thing: "every knee shall bow to me, and every tongue shall confess to God."

Verse 12, one more time: **"So then every one of us shall give account of himself to God."** Don't worry about person A, B or C. Just worry about yourself. Because one day, you will stand in the presence of Almighty God and He will judge you. He will judge you thoroughly. Every word, thought and deed. So, stop interfering in the lives of other people. Just focus on your own walk with the Lord Jesus Christ.

**VERSES 13-15: "Let us not therefore judge one another any more: but judge this rather, that no man put a stumblingblock or an occasion to fall in *his* brother's way.**

**I know, and am persuaded by the Lord Jesus, that *there is* nothing unclean of itself: but to him that esteemeth any thing to be unclean, to him *it is* unclean. But if thy brother be grieved with *thy* meat, now walkest thou not charitably. Destroy not him with thy meat, for whom Christ died."**

Verses 13 down to 15 are very clear, and I showed you last time how some of the early Christians, before they got saved, would worship, not only animals but also false gods, and part of their sacrifice was to present food to these false deities. And so Paul, being ever so aware of this, warns those that were stronger in the faith not to cause those that were weaker to stumble or to become offended, and he says in verse 14 to those who esteemed something to be unclean, to them it is unclean.

But we know, those that are stronger in the faith, that there is nothing unclean of itself. To the pure, all things are pure. And so by verse 15, he says: **"But if thy brother be grieved with *thy* meat, now walkest thou not charitably. Destroy not him with thy meat, for whom Christ died."** Don't defile his conscience. Be careful what you do. Enjoy your liberty in Christ, yes! But not at the expense of a weaker brother or sister. Because if you do so, the Lord God is going to hold you accountable at the Judgment Seat of Christ.

**VERSES 16-17: "Let not then your good be evil spoken of: For the kingdom of God is not meat and drink; but righteousness, and peace, and joy in the Holy Ghost."**

The Holy Ghost, of course, is the Holy Spirit. How else could you have peace and joy if He's not God? He, of course, is a third

Member of the Godhead. The Kingdom of God is also the same of the Kingdom of Heaven. And yet saying that, please allow me to say this: for those of us alive today, we are in the spiritual realm of the Kingdom of God. But for those that have died, they are in the physical realm. And we saw that from verse 9, how He, Christ, might be Lord both of the dead and living! So the Holy Ghost is the Holy Spirit, and the Kingdom of God is the Kingdom of Heaven.

**VERSES 18-19: "For he that in these things serveth Christ *is* acceptable to God, and approved of men. Let us therefore follow after the things which make for peace, and things wherewith one may edify another."**

So the Kingdom of God, for those of us alive today, is not about food or drink. It's not even about money. Please turn to Psalm 49. And nor is it about power or prestige. Take a look, please, at verse 10: **"For he seeth *that* wise men die, likewise the fool and the brutish person perish, and leave their wealth to others. Their inward thought *is, that* their houses *shall continue* for ever, and their dwelling places to all generations; they call *their* lands after their own names. Nevertheless man *being* in honour abideth not: he is like the beasts *that* perish."**

So please turn back to Romans chapter 14. So, the Kingdom of God, one more time, is not about meat or drink. And neither is it about money, power or prestige. It's all about God. And finally, verse 19, one more time: **"let us therefore follow after the things which make for peace, and things wherewith one may edify another."** Deny yourself, and put others first!

**VERSES 20-23:** **"For meat destroy not the work of God. All things indeed *are* pure; but *it is* evil for that man who eateth with offence. *It is* good neither to eat flesh, nor to drink wine, nor *any thing* whereby thy brother stumbleth, or is offended, or is made weak. Hast thou faith? have *it* to thyself before God. Happy *is* he that condemneth not himself in that thing which he alloweth. And he that doubteth is damned if he eat, because *he eateth* not of faith: for whatsoever *is* not of faith is sin."**

I think it's fair to call the 14th chapter the "Chapter of Liberty." You can do whatever you wish to do, providing you don't cause someone else to stumble. And at the same time, if a saved person falls into sin, you can still approach them and call them to repent, Matthew chapter 18.

But this chapter, one final time, is focusing primarily on the liberty that all born-again Bible-believing Christians can enjoy. You can worship the Lord on whatever day of the week you care to do so. You can eat whatever you choose to eat as well. But just be careful and mindful not to invade someone else's liberty. Don't be a pharisee. Rest in the finished work of the Lord Jesus Christ, and allow your brethren to make their own decisions in this life.

# CHAPTER 15

---

Chapter 15, verses 1-3: "We then that are strong ought to bear the infirmities of the weak, and not to please ourselves. Let every one of us please *his* neighbour for *his* good to edification. For even Christ pleased not himself; but, as it is written, The reproaches of them that reproached thee fell on me."

Verses 1 to 3 continue on from chapter 14 in reference to how we that are stronger in the faith ought to carry those that are weaker in the faith.

And I showed you last time how one of the main problems that some of the early Christians were still experiencing were convicted consciences. Some of them, before they were saved, would worship false gods and even animals. And once they got saved they were still battling their old natures.

For them, food was still a sore subject. And the apostle Paul, ever so mindful of this, told those that were stronger in the faith not to cause those that were weaker in the faith to stumble. And so Paul says how we are not to please ourselves, but we are to please our neighbours. First of all we are expected to bear the infirmities of our brethren, and then we are expected to please our neighbours.

The Lord God is not willing that any should perish, but that all should come to repentance. And so, as ambassadors for Christ, we are never off duty. Let your light shine before the world!

In verse 3, the apostle Paul holds up the Lord Jesus Christ as a personification of self-denial and self-sacrifice: **"For even Christ pleased not himself; but, as it is written, The reproaches of them that reproached thee fell on me."** So, be Christ-like and deny yourself, and at the same time be available to the weaker brethren, and at the same time reach out to your unsaved neighbours. Present the gospel to them.

**VERSE 4: "For whatsoever things were written aforetime were written for our learning, that we through patience and comfort of the scriptures might have hope."**

Hope in God and hope in the word of God. No matter how bad things get, we have the Scriptures and we have God. But above all, we can use these things to comfort one another. We are here for one another. **"Faith without works is dead"** (James 2:26).

And even though I showed you last time, from Romans chapter 8, how we are eternally secure in the Lord Jesus Christ (once saved always saved, or if saved, always saved), trials and tribulations are always going to be a part of everyday life. And the reason for this, of course, is two-fold. Number one: to prune us, to humble us, to allow us to produce more fruit and to become holier. And number two: to be able to reach out to one another, to be able to understand one another's infirmities and weaknesses and problems.

**VERSES 5-7:** "Now the God of patience and consolation grant you to be likeminded one toward another according to Christ Jesus: That ye may with one mind *and* one mouth glorify God, even the Father of our Lord Jesus Christ. Wherefore receive ye one another, as Christ also received us to the glory of God."

Verse 5: **"be likeminded one toward another"** and by verse 6: be of one mind and one mouth when it comes to glorifying God. There will always be divisions in the body of Christ. There is nothing new under the sun. But here the apostle Paul makes it very clear how we should all be likeminded one toward another, because divisions when it comes to our worship of Him only cause dishonour and disunity. So, pray for one another and be there for one another. But above all, keep God at the centre of everything that you do.

**VERSES 8-12:** "Now I say that Jesus Christ was a minister of the circumcision for the truth of God, to confirm the promises *made* unto the fathers: And that the Gentiles might glorify God for *his* mercy; as it is written, For this cause I will confess to thee among the Gentiles, and sing unto thy name. And again he saith, Rejoice, ye Gentiles, with his people. And again, Praise the Lord, all ye Gentiles; and laud him, all ye people. And again, Esaias saith, There shall be a root of Jesse, and he that shall rise to reign over the Gentiles; in him shall the Gentiles trust."

Verse 8, Jesus is called a minister of the circumcision, meaning the Jews, of course. And the word "minister" simply means a servant. He was never ordained by anyone in organised religion. He came to fulfil the law and to confirm the promises made unto the fathers: Abraham, Isaac and Jacob.

And from verses 9 down to 12, the term "Gentiles" appears six times: It was always the Lord's will to reach out to the Gentiles and save them. John 10, verse 16, the Lord Jesus Christ speaking: **"And other sheep I have, which are not of this fold: them also I must bring, and they shall hear my voice; and there shall be one fold, *and* one shepherd."** These other sheep are, of course, the Gentiles that were going to believe on Him after the resurrection. And once they did so, they, too, would be added into His one fold. One Church, one baptism, one faith, one body of Christ.

Isaiah 49, verse 1: **"The LORD hath called me from the womb; from the bowels of my mother hath he made mention of my name." Verse 5: "And now, saith the LORD that formed me from the womb *to be* his servant, to bring Jacob again to him. Though Israel be not gathered, yet shall I be glorious in the eyes of the LORD, and my God shall be my strength. And he said, it is a light thing that thou shouldest be my servant to raise up the tribes of Jacob, and to restore the preserved of Israel: I will also give thee for a light to the Gentiles, that thou mayest be my salvation unto the end of the earth."**

"Jesus" in Hebrew means "Yeshua", and "Yeshua" means salvation, found here in verse 6, written by Isaiah, 700 B.C., concerning God the Father speaking to God the Son.

**VERSES 13-16: "Now the God of hope fill you with all joy and peace in believing, that ye may abound in hope, through the power of the Holy Ghost. And I myself also am persuaded of you, my brethren, that ye also are full of goodness, filled with all knowledge, able also to admonish one another. Nevertheless, brethren, I have written the more boldly unto you in some sort, as putting you in mind, because of the grace that is given to me of God, That I should be the minister of Jesus Christ to the Gentiles, ministering the gospel of God, that the offering up of the Gentiles might be acceptable, being sanctified by the Holy Ghost."**

Verse 13: **"Now the God of hope fill you with all joy and peace in believing, that ye may abound in hope through the power of the Holy Ghost."** He wants you to grow in grace. Faith comes by hearing, and hearing by the word of God (Romans 10:17). The more Bible you read, the greater you grow in grace. And the more you grow in grace, the greater your faith will be. You will believe the Bible at a much deeper level.

Verse 16, Paul says, **"That I should be the minister of Jesus Christ to the Gentiles."** Verse 8, Jesus is called **"a minister of the circumcision"**, in reference, of course, to the Jews. But here Paul is saying how he is also a minister, but this time, to the Gentiles. A minister simply meaning a servant, no more than a servant.

And also from verse 14, Paul says how he was persuaded that the brethren were full of all goodness, filled with all knowledge, able also to admonish one another. They weren't sinless, of course, but they were filled with all knowledge of God, because of verse 13, they were filled with all joy and peace by believing in the Lord Jesus Christ, by believing in the word of God, and therefore they were able to humbly admonish one another.

**VERSES 17-19:** "**I have therefore whereof I may glory through Jesus Christ in those things which pertain to God. For I will not dare to speak of any of those things which Christ hath not wrought by me, to make the Gentiles obedient, by word and deed, Through mighty signs and wonders, by the power of the Spirit of God; so that from Jerusalem, and round about unto Illyricum, I have fully preached the gospel of Christ.**"

Verse 18 is so very clear, the apostles, including Paul, of course, only told mankind what the Lord God of the Bible had told them. Their writings were inspired. The Bible, therefore, is the word of God, and you can trust it 100%. On top of that he came in the power and with the authority of the Holy Spirit. He raised the dead. He wrote half of the New Testament. He went to the third Heaven, and yet he was never filled with pride. He walked in submission to the Lord God of the Bible, and the Lord God used him above all of the apostles. And his ministry and his gospel totally transformed the world.

**VERSES 20-21:** "**Yea, so have I strived to preach the gospel, not where Christ was named, lest I should build upon another man's foundation: But as it is written, To whom he was not spoken of, they shall see: and they that have not heard shall understand.**"

Verse 20 makes it so very clear how the apostle Paul was not prepared to preach the gospel or build upon another man's foundation, meaning he was not prepared to go to Rome if the apostle Peter, or the apostle John, or the apostle James were already there.

But clearly we know from chapter 1, verse 7, how the apostle Paul was writing: **"To all that be in Rome, beloved of God, called *to be* saints: Grace to you and peace from God our Father, and the Lord Jesus Christ."** Clearly there were already a well-established group of Bible-believing Christians in Rome, around the time that he wrote this epistle, which is about 56 A.D. And so this whole epistle, written by the apostle Paul in Corinth, is really his desire, his stopgap. He's telling the people of Rome: I'm going to come to you. Verse 11: **"For I long to see you, that I may impart unto you some spiritual gift."**

So, one more time, the apostle Paul, the apostle John, and the apostle James had not reached Rome. Is it possible they may have travelled through Rome? Yes, that is possible.

But the main point, I believe, from verse 15:20, is how Paul was not prepared to build upon another man's foundation. Peter, James and John were not in Rome. Peter may have travelled through Rome possibly, like I say, but he was not a permanent fixture in Rome. Rome was not his base, it was going to be Paul's base, and Paul was martyred in Rome, whereas Peter, I believe, was martyred in either Jerusalem or Babylon.

And verse 21 makes it very clear to me, **"To whom he was not spoken of, they shall see: and they that have not heard shall**

**understand."** The apostles had not yet made it to Rome. The apostle Paul was the first apostle, I believe, to make it to Rome. Yes, there were early believers in Rome. Acts chapter 18, like I say, would explain how these early Christians got started, but verse 21 makes it clear to me how the apostle Paul was the first apostle to make it to Rome.

**VERSES 22-25: "For which cause also I have been much hindered from coming to you. But now having no more place in these parts, and having a great desire these many years to come unto you; Whensoever I take my journey into Spain, I will come to you: for I trust to see you in my journey, and to be brought on my way thitherward by you, if first I be somewhat filled with your *company*. But now I go unto Jerusalem to minister unto the saints."**

For most of the apostle Paul's life, he was buffeted by the devil. He was told back in Acts chapter 9 how he would suffer terribly for the glory of God.

So, if you are born again, if you are living for the Lord God of the Bible, you too, are going to be buffeted. You'll be tried and tested. But please, always remember this from 1 Corinthians chapter 10, verse 13: **"There hath no temptation taken you but such as is common to man: but God *is* faithful, who will not suffer you to be tempted above that ye are able; but will with the temptation also make a way to escape, that ye may be able to bear *it*."**

Clearly, it's no surprise that the devil would not want Paul to arrive in Rome. Because Paul knew if he could make it in

Rome, he could make it anywhere. And from Rome he could, and would, eventually transform the world for the Lord Jesus Christ.

**Chapter 15, verses 26-33: "For it hath pleased them of Macedonia and Achaia to make a certain contribution for the poor saints which are at Jerusalem. It hath pleased them verily; and their debtors they are. For if the Gentiles have been made partakers of their spiritual things, their duty is also to minister unto them in carnal things. When therefore I have performed this, and have sealed to them this fruit, I will come by you into Spain. And I am sure that, when I come unto you, I shall come in the fulness of the blessing of the gospel of Christ. Now I beseech you, brethren, for the Lord Jesus Christ's sake, and for the love of the Spirit, that ye strive together with me in *your* prayers to God for me; That I may be delivered from them that do not believe in Judaea; and that my service which *I have* for Jerusalem may be accepted of the saints; That I may come unto you with joy by the will of God, and may with you be refreshed. Now the God of peace *be* with you all. Amen."**

Verse 26, the Gentiles at Macedonia and Achaia made a certain contribution to the poor Jews which were at Jerusalem. The Gentiles on this occasion were supporting their Jewish brethren. **"Faith without works is dead".**

Romans 15:30, he says, **"I beseech you brethren,"** I beg you brothers and sisters, **"for the Lord Jesus Christ's sake and for the love of the Spirit, that ye strive together with me in your prayers to God for me."** That's intercession with a capital "I".

And the latter part of verse 30, he **says "for the love of the Spirit,"** the Spirit being the Holy Ghost, of course. And you were told to **"love the Lord thy God with all thy heart, and with all thy soul, and with all thy mind, and with all thy strength"** (Mark 12:30).

Also verses 26 and 31 are joined up. First of all, in reference to verse 26, there were many poor saints in the early church, Jews and Gentiles. This message that we hear so much of today, this so-called "prosperity message" where God wants you to be healthy and wealthy, was not something that the early church ever believed or taught or ever experienced. There was great poverty, like I say, in the early church. And the apostle Paul is quite rightly commending the Gentiles that stepped in to support their Jewish brethren.

Secondly, from verse 31, the apostle Paul wants the Romans to pray for him. Why? Because the Jews wanted to kill him, as did the Gentiles on some occasions, because the gospel and his ministry, specifically, were an offence to mankind, especially the Judaizers.

But we were told in chapter 11 to pray for the Jews nevertheless, because they are beloved for their father's sakes: Abraham, Isaac and Jacob.

So Paul, as always, was selfless. He was the best of the best. He was the prince of the apostles. But pride was not something he ever battled with. So from Jerusalem to Spain, from Spain to Malta, and from Malta to Rome, the apostle Paul is on his way.

But before he arrives in Rome, he concludes, chapter 15 one more time, verse 33: **"Now the God of peace *be* with you all. Amen."** P-E-A-C-E. "We have peace with God through our Lord Jesus Christ" (Romans 5:1). Amen and amen.

# CHAPTER 16

**V**ERSES 1-4: "I commend unto you Phebe our sister, which is a servant of the church which is at Cenchrea: That ye receive her in the Lord, as becometh saints, and that ye assist her in whatsoever business she hath need of you: for she hath been a succourer of many, and of myself also. Greet Priscilla and Aquila my helpers in Christ Jesus: Who have for my life laid down their own necks: unto whom not only I give thanks, but also all the churches of the Gentiles."

Phebe, from verse 1, was a servant. She was not an apostle, she was not a disciple, she was not an elder, and she was not a pastor. She was just a servant, much like you found in the last chapter. The Lord Jesus Christ was a servant of the circumcision, and the apostle Paul was a servant of the Gentiles. But whoever she was, she was of great importance, because the apostle Paul commends her unto the church, and he says to them, **"receive her in the Lord, as becometh saints".**

And he goes on to praise "Priscilla and Aquila my helpers in Christ Jesus: Who have for my life laid down their own necks: unto whom not only I give thanks, but also all the churches of the Gentiles." And he also says about Priscilla and Aquila, **"my helpers in Christ Jesus: who have for my life laid down their own necks."** They too, were prepared to die, not only for the Lord Jesus Christ but also for the apostle Paul. It cost something for the early church to not only be Christians, but to also be associated with men like the apostle Paul. They, too, were prepared to die for the cause of the gospel. And he says also, in the latter part of verse 4: **"unto whom not only I give thanks, but also all the churches of the Gentiles."** This couple were magnificent!

**VERSES 5-7: "Likewise *greet* the church that is in their house. Salute my wellbeloved Epaenetus, who is of the firstfruits of Achaia unto Christ. Greet Mary, who bestowed much labour on us. Salute Andronicus and Junia, my kinsmen, and my fellowprisoners, who are of note among the apostles, who also were in Christ before me."**

Verse 5 is a continuation from verses 3 and 4. Priscilla and Aquila had a church which met in their home. The early church met in the homes for the most part. Church buildings, as we know them today, evolved over decades and centuries. Some of the early church were Jewish and they would meet in their synagogues, but for the most part, the early church, being Gentiles, met in people's homes.

Verse 6, this Mary was not the mother of the Lord Jesus Christ. She was quite possibly a lady of status, like Lydia, like Phebe and like Dorcas. And also, to any Roman Catholic that may be listening to this broadcast, the Roman Catholic Church, as you know, elevates Mary to a great position of power and authority and prestige. And here, the apostle Paul is listing Mary in fourth place. So could this really be the queen of heaven listed here in fourth place? I don't believe so. In Acts chapter 1, doctor Luke lists Mary, the mother of the Lord Jesus Christ, in 13th place. Nobody ever consulted her on anything.

But this Mary, in Romans 16:6 **"bestowed much labour on us."** She was like Mary and Martha, she was greatly beloved by the early church, and verse 7, **"Andronicus and Junia, my kinsmen and fellowprisoners, who are of note among the apostles, who also were in Christ before me,"** they got saved before Paul got saved, proving here that everyone gets saved the moment they believe on the Lord Jesus Christ. No one has been chosen before the foundation of the world. They got saved before Paul got saved. This husband-and-wife team were known among the apostles, but they were not apostles. They were simply of note among the apostles. But above all, they were in Christ before the apostle Paul was in Christ.

**VERSES 8-16:** "**Greet Amplias my beloved in the Lord. Salute Urbane, our helper in Christ, and Stachys my beloved. Salute Apelles approved in Christ. Salute them which are of Aristobulus'** *household*. **Salute Herodion my kinsman. Greet them that be of the** *household* **of Narcissus, which are in the Lord. Salute Tryphena and Tryphosa, who labour in the Lord. Salute the beloved Persis, which laboured much in the Lord. Salute Rufus chosen in the Lord, and his mother and mine. Salute Asyncritus, Phlegon, Hermas, Patrobas, Hermes, and the brethren which are with them. Salute Philologus, and Julia, Nereus, and his sister, and Olympas, and all the saints which are with them. Salute one another with an holy kiss. The churches of Christ salute you.**"

Verses 8 down to 16 continues a drumroll when it comes to the apostle Paul paying homage to the best of the best in Rome.

Also of interest to me in reference to Priscilla and Aquila, this husband-and-wife team, were how monumental they were in leading Apollos, from Acts chapter 18, out from the law and into grace. This is very much what the apostle Paul is doing not only in Romans, but also in Galatians. The Old Testament for the Jews, the New Testament for the Gentiles.

Many of the Jews were not sure where they now fitted in to the New Covenant, and people like Priscilla and Aquila, this amazing husband-and-wife team, were used mightily by the Holy Ghost, and that's why the apostle Paul, I believe, is quite rightly commending this couple in the Lord to the brethren. And no doubt these were leaders of house churches.

And he finishes in verse 16 to salute on another with a holy kiss. And the meaning of this term, a holy kiss, is very simply, the kissing of friends on the forehead, cheek or beard. It was something that was very common in the Old Testament, and so the Jewish believers in the Lord Jesus Christ continued it on, and quite possibly the Gentile believers also adopted this as well.

And I'll close this broadcast, if I may, from Psalm 85, to show you the innocence of this holy kiss. Verse 10: **"Mercy and truth are met together; righteousness and peace have kissed *each other."***

**VERSES 17-19: "Now I beseech you, brethren, mark them which cause divisions and offences contrary to the doctrine which ye have learned; and avoid them. For they that are such serve not our Lord Jesus Christ, but their own belly;**

**and by good words and fair speeches deceive the hearts of the simple. For your obedience is come abroad unto all men. I am glad therefore on your behalf: but yet I would have you wise unto that which is good, and simple concerning evil."**

Verses 17 down to 19 are the apostle Paul's final warning to the Romans, and vicariously everyone else. Be careful, he is telling you, to mark them which cause divisions and offences which are contrary to the doctrine which ye have learned, and avoid them.

What is the doctrine of Christ? I believe the doctrine of Christ is very simply how **"the just shall live by faith."** You were saved by your faith in the Lord Jesus Christ. Grace alone, faith alone, Christ alone.

Also from verse 17 you were told to avoid them, in reference, of course, to false teachers. In Galatians chapter 1, Paul said that if anyone or anything would come to you in the name of the Lord Jesus Christ, preaching or offering another gospel, something that was not substantiated by the apostles, they are to be cursed. And the same is found here in verse 17: mark those that cause divisions and offences, that are contrary to the doctrine which you have learned, and avoid them.

So the doctrine of the Lord Jesus Christ, one more time, is how you are saved by your faith in Christ alone. Grace alone, faith alone, Christ alone.

And furthermore, in reference to false teachers, the New Testament also tells us how we are to expose all workers of iniquity, and how we are also expected to rebuke them sharply in the Lord Jesus Christ. In verse 18, Paul tells us how these people don't serve the **"Lord Jesus Christ but their own belly, and by good words and fair speeches, deceive the hearts of the simple,"** in reference of course to those that are not educated in the deeper things of the Lord God.

One more time, people like Priscilla and Aquila were marvellous in that they were able to articulate the simplicity of the Lord Jesus Christ.

And also from verse 18, he makes the very interesting comment how they don't serve the Lord Jesus, but their own belly. Not necessarily in reference to their obesity, but more likely in reference to their lack of self-control. And he goes on to say how they do this by their good words and fair speeches. This, therefore, is a philosophical problem, not a theological one. And verse 19, one more time: the apostle Paul, not only wearing his heart on his sleeve, but here wanting to prepare and present the bride of Christ as a chaste virgin to the Lord Jesus Christ, **"I would have you wise unto that which is good, and simple concerning evil."**

So take verses 17 down to 19, and we come to the following conclusion: verse 17, **"mark them which cause divisions and offences contrary to the doctrine which ye have learned, and avoid them."** Why? Because God is going to punish such people. He has reserved a special place in Hell for all false teachers and all false teachings.

In verse 18, they (the false teachers) **"serve not our Lord Jesus, but their own belly, and by good words and fair speeches, deceive the hearts of the simple."** Not in reference to somebody being stupid, but more in reference to somebody not necessarily understanding the deeper things of Scripture. Hence, why you were told to read the word of God each and every day, and meditate on the word of God each and every day. And on verse 19, be wise, be aware, be mindful unto that which is good, but simple. Don't practice, don't be a partaker of that which concerns evil.

**VERSE 20: "And the God of peace shall bruise Satan under your feet shortly. The grace of our Lord Jesus Christ be with you. Amen."**

Verse 20 is very much in conclusion to verses 17 down to 19. The devil is the archenemy of anything that is pro-God and anyone that is pro-Christ. His job is to destroy the saints, and he does that in many different ways, but the main way that he does this is by false teachings and false teachers.

Please turn to Psalm 58. Like I said last time, I believe the Lord God of the Bible has reserved a special place in Hell for all false teachers, and of course for the wicked in general. But please take a look at Psalm 58, verse 10: **"The righteous shall rejoice when he seeth the vengeance: he shall wash his feet in the blood of the wicked. So that a man shall say, Verily *there is* a reward for the righteous: verily he is a God that judgeth in the earth."**

Please turn to Psalm 75 and take a look at verse 8: **"For in the hand of the LORD** *there is* **a cup, and the wine is red; it is full of mixture; and he poureth out of the same: but the dregs thereof, all the wicked of the earth shall wring** *them* **out,** *and* **drink** *them.***"**

Please turn back to Romans chapter 16 and verse 20 one more time: **"And the God of peace shall bruise Satan under your feet shortly. The grace of our Lord Jesus Christ** *be* **with you. Amen."**

So, when we take all of these verses together, from Romans chapter 16, Psalm 58 and Psalm 75, we discover how the Lord God is going to punish, he is going to destroy not only the wicked but also Satan under our feet shortly. But in the meantime, we have been told to mark those that cause divisions and offences which are contrary to the doctrine of Christ. Mark them out, warn others, and avoid them.

**VERSES 21-23: "Timotheus my workfellow, and Lucius, and Jason, and Sosipater, my kinsmen, salute you. I Tertius, who wrote** *this* **epistle, salute you in the Lord. Gaius mine host, and of the whole church, saluteth you. Erastus the chamberlain of the city saluteth you, and Quartus a brother."**

So verses 21 down to 24 are Paul's final drumroll of the righteous. This is very much a picture of the Judgment Seat of Christ, when the Lord Jesus Christ reads out all of the names of the righteous. But here, Paul is praising and crediting the good and the great. In verse 22, Tertius wrote this epistle, why?

Because Paul suffered from poor eyesight. This epistle is still inspired by the Holy Ghost, the apostle Paul simply spoke the epistle to Tertius, who wrote it down, and Paul entrusted Phebe to take the Epistle of the Romans, via Corinth, to Rome.

And verse 24 feeds back in to the latter part of verse 20. **Verse 24: "The grace of our Lord Jesus Christ *be* with you all. Amen."**

**VERSES 25-27: "Now to him that is of power to stablish you according to my gospel, and the preaching of Jesus Christ, according to the revelation of the mystery, which was kept secret since the world began, But now is made manifest, and by the scriptures of the prophets, according to the commandment of the everlasting God, made known to all nations for the obedience of faith: To God only wise, *be* glory through Jesus Christ for ever. Amen."**

From verse 25, Paul speaks about the mystery, which was kept secret since the world began. Ultimately, he is referring to the ministry of the Lord Jesus Christ. From Abraham to Malachi, the Jews (for the most part) had a very primitive understanding as to who the Lord God of the Bible was, so it fell to the apostles and especially Paul to write the New Testament and present the Lord Jesus Christ to the world.

This mystery, which had been kept secret from eternity past, has now been revealed under the New Covenant, and so every book of the New Testament is God's revelation to the world concerning His Son, the Lord Jesus Christ.

And verse 25, the apostle Paul, says **"Now to him** [God] **that is of power to establish you according to my gospel."** Do you want to know the Lord God? Get down on your knees and say, "God, please be merciful to me, a sinner" and He will save you the moment you cry out to Him. If you are saved but out of fellowship with the Lord God of the Bible, get down on your knees and say, "Lord God, please be merciful to me, a sinner." And He will restore you. He will give you the power to make this book come alive one more time for you.

And also from verse 26, he says, "according to the commandment of the everlasting God, made known to all nations for the obedience of faith." God the Father is eternal, God the Son is eternal, and God the Holy Spirit is eternal too. So when you sin against God, only God Himself can forgive you. And because God is eternal, you are going to be eternal as well. You will either be in Heaven with the Lord Jesus Christ, or you will be in Hell for all of eternity. Take this book very seriously, please. This is not a game.

And the latter part of verse 26: **"made known to all nations for the obedience of faith."** One more time: **"we walk by faith, not by sight."** You were saved by your faith in the Lord Jesus Christ. It's all about God. He makes it possible for all men to be saved, but only those that believe on Him are actually going to be saved.

So, what started back in verse 1, with Phebe being commissioned and entrusted to travel from Corinth to Rome with the Epistle of the Romans, is now found here in verse 26: for the obedience of faith to all nations. So, not only were many people saved in Rome, but they were also saved in Ephesus and Corinth, and in Galatia. The entire world was turned upside down by the power of the Lord Jesus Christ.

So give God the glory and the praise. It's all about Him. And verse 27, one more time: **"To God only wise, *be* glory through Jesus Christ for ever. Amen."** So, this verse will conclude my unscripted Bible study of the Epistle to the Romans, I recorded this primarily for Ex-Catholics For Christ radio. This series of recordings lasts just under 7 hours. So, thank you for starting with me, for continuing with me, and for finishing with me. And I commend this epistle to the Lord God of the Bible. Amen and amen.

# Also by James Battell

The Shocking History of the Jesuits (The Society of Jesus)
King James I of England: The King The Vatican Could Not
Kill
The Hidden Truth About Freemasonry, The Catholic Church,
And The Illuminati
Bible Prophecy Made Simple For Serious Students of
Scripture
Did The Catholic Church Order Abraham Lincoln's
Assassination?
Is Calvinism and the Doctrines of Grace Biblical?
The Book of Genesis Commentary (Chapters 1-11)
The Book of Genesis Commentary (Chapters 1-11)
Watchman Nee, Witness Lee, and Living Stream Ministry: A
Critical Analysis of Their Identity as Cult or Church
What Is Speaking In Tongues And Is It Still For Today?
Ephesians KJV Bible Commentary
The Book of Romans Commentary
Philemon Bible Study (Slavery In Scripture)
Turbulent Thrones: Charles vs. Cromwell's Epic Struggle for
England's Soul
The Holy Ghost Within The Trinity
Papal Infallibility or Insanity?
The Immaculate Conception ("Deception")